BUSH WARFARE

BUSH WARFARE

BY
LIEUT.-COLONEL W. C. G. HENEKER, D.S.O.
(Connaught Rangers)

The Naval & Military Press Ltd

Published by

The Naval & Military Press Ltd
Unit 5 Riverside, Brambleside
Bellbrook Industrial Estate
Uckfield, East Sussex
TN22 1QQ England

Tel: +44 (0)1825 749494

www.naval-military-press.com
www.nmarchive.com

In reprinting in facsimile from the original, any imperfections are inevitably reproduced and the quality may fall short of modern type and cartographic standards.

CONTENTS.

		PAGE
Chapter I.	Tactics	1
,, II.	Size and Composition of Columns	60
,, III.	Transport and Supplies	86
,, IV.	Unit, the Section	115
,, V.	Artillery and Machine Guns	120
,, VI.	Marches	127
,, VII.	Encampments and their Safeguard	131
,, VIII.	Night Operations	140
,, IX.	Subjugation of a Country	147
,, X.	Levies	167
,, XI.	Information and Reconnaissance	181
,, XII.	Communication	186
,, XIII.	Relief of Towns	190
,, XIV.	Political Officers	195

PLANS.

Plan No. 1.—Okoroji's Farm. Aro Campaign, 1901-2		8
,, 2.—Square Formation. Bida-Ilorin Expedition		34
,, 3.—Afikpo Expedition, 1902-3		35
,, 4.—Battle of Jidballi		38
,, 5.—Battle on the Monongahela (A)		48
,, 6.— Do. do. (B)		50
,, 7.—Achin War, 1874		61
,, 8.—Benin Expedition, 1897		66
,, 9.—German S. W. Africa		76
,, 10.—Waterberg Fight		78
,, 11.—Brohemie Town and Creek		84
,, 12.—Esuitu Creek Camp		134
,, 13.—Aro Expedition, 1901-2		160

PREFACE

SHOULD any officer, about to essay his first attempt at bush fighting, happen to peruse these notes, and should he, perchance, come across anything which may be of use to him, the following pages will have served the purpose for which they were written.

The bush warfare referred to here is principally West African. Fighting in other parts of the world in enclosed terrain has only been touched upon superficially.

A great many of the incidents recorded are personal experiences, but a large number also have been taken from published despatches, as well as from the books and works of men who have placed their adventures, experiences, and conclusions on paper.

I have endeavoured not to lay down, for formations and tactics, hard and fast rules which I consider *ought to be adhered to*. Such a proceeding would not only be against the teachings of warfare, but would manifestly be absurd.

The attempt has been made to describe methods which have been successful in the past, and should the conditions under which they were found to be efficacious suffer a change, it will only be reasonable and right that the commander of the future should modify and alter them to suit the situation which may confront him.

My thanks are due to Colonel G. V. Kemball, C.B., D.S.O., late Inspector-General West African Frontier Force, for his advice and assistance; and also to various other officers who have been good enough to send me information on certain points.

W. C. G. HENEKER, Lieut.-Col.

Bloemfontein, August 22, 1906.

BUSH WARFARE.

CHAPTER I.

Tactics.

WITHIN the last few years the methods of carrying on warfare against savages have completely changed. Up to that time, with few exceptions, the white man depended entirely on luck, pluck and a superior weapon. Columns of soldiers in single file moved silently along the bush paths in the half light of the dense forests, every nerve strained almost to breaking. At any moment the roar and flash of the dane guns on all sides might disclose an ambush, and it then became the duty of the survivors on the bush path to wipe out the hidden enemy. Sections or sub-sections turned right and left alternately and, under their commanders, riddled the bush, at the height of three feet from the ground, with volleys. Sometimes the enemy gave way at once; at others, posted in trenches or behind stockades, he held out for a considerable time, and managed to inflict grievous loss on the concentrated and exposed groups of soldiery. The dense smoke from the enemy's guns, fired off at a distance of a few yards from the path, hung in the

Past Methods.

bush on the moisture-laden atmosphere and made it impossible to see more than a few yards. The flashes of the guns, the yells and tom-tomming of the enemy, and the shouts of the various commanders directing the fire and encouraging their men, combined to make an 'inferno' which tried the strongest nerves, and made it impossible for a commander to do anything but encourage those immediately about him. General supervision was impossible, combined movements or action was not attempted. The maxims and 7 pounders were brought up and opened on those portions of the bush from which the greatest noise came. Their fire gradually cut away the leaves and lighter parts of the dense foliage, and, by driving the smoke back, disclosed the positions of the enemy, who probably now had had enough of it, and, retiring precipitately to another prepared position, lay in wait again for the confiding white man. The rule was now to advance, firing clearing, or covering volleys. A certain number of men were told off for this duty, and halting every 50 or 100 yards fired one or more volleys into the bush on each side of the path in the direction of the advance. This nearly always had the effect of disclosing an ambush before the troops got into the middle of it, and consequently the dane guns were not so effective, and rarely carried farther than the leading troops of the column. The same procedure as before was then adopted of bringing up the guns and firing blindly into the bush. The carrier column was protected by placing groups of men at regular intervals throughout the column, and these groups fired promiscuous volleys into the bush on either flank, and so kept the enemy from crawling up and choosing their victims as they stood quietly awaiting a continuation of the advance. Many a white

Clearing Volleys.

man and carrier, however, lost his life by getting a charge of slugs into him from a distance of a few yards, owing to some extra brave savage lying flat behind a log and awaiting his chance, secure in the knowledge that the covering volley would go over his head. The soldier remained on the bush path ; had he been allowed to enter the bush, it was feared he would get out of hand.

It will be seen how trying this mode of carrying on bush warfare was to the nerves, and how prodigal in the matter of ammunition, enormous quantities of which had to be carried in comparison to the number of troops engaged.

At the commencement of the 1900 Ashanti Campaign, one column, consisting of a 7-pounder gun, two maxims and 250 men, was ordered to the relief of Kumassi. They were very roughly handled by the Ashantis, who did all they could to retard the advance. Through the splendid qualities of the five British officers, all of whom were wounded, the Ashantis were defeated, but little more than 100 sound men arrived in Kumassi, with only 9,000 rounds. Their casualties thus amounted to about 60 per cent., they had expended and lost in the bush something like 80,000 rounds, and another day's fighting would have meant disaster, owing to lack of ammunition.

On its arrival it could hardly be called a relieving column, but this was not the fault of its commander, who obeyed his orders in hurrying to Kumassi. The short story of this shattered force is one of splendid courage and determination.

Again, at Dompoassi 400 men fired 40,000 rounds in $2\frac{1}{2}$ hours, and effected nothing, and it was only as a last resource that the charge of the Yoruba Company under Colour-Sergt. Mackenzie (now Lieut. Mackenzie, V.C.) was undertaken, and succeeded in at once dislodging the Ashantis, who had up to that time held a secure position behind a strong stockade.

During the Sierra Leone rebellion of 1898, a force was held up in a place called Karina. A detachment moved out to a district some miles away, but adopting the system of clearing volleys, expended so much ammunition that it had to return to Karina, and this retirement and failure of the offensive movement was at that juncture most unfortunate.

Precautionary or covering volleys were used exclusively in the 1897 Benin Expedition, and the expenditure of ammunition was very heavy.

It was also used in the Benin Territories Expedition of 1899, and the ammunition supply gave more anxiety, and needed more carriers, than it now does under the scouting method of disclosing an enemy's ambush.

During the reconnaissance of the country round Okemue, Ologboshiri's chief town, 35 men, a maxim gun, and a rocket tube were detailed one day to reconnoitre along the principal path which led to the town. The enemy's scouts barred the way, and had to be driven in. Precautionary volleys by four or five men only were used to clear the bush. The reconnaissance up to the town was effected, but it was found then that ammunition was running short. The force retired, was harassed all the way for nearly three miles, and had it not been for the expedient adopted by the rearguard of laying an ambush, which checked the ardour of the exultant pursuers, the party might not have got away intact. On arrival in camp it was found that three rounds of S.A. ammunition remained ; on starting, each man had been served out with 100 rounds.

As in every class of warfare, and against all

nations, we cannot hope to bring matters to a satisfactory conclusion until the enemy's forces in the field have suffered severe defeat. The capture and burning of towns is, of course, a concomitant to savage fighting ; but if, in the taking of these places, the enemy has not been made to suffer severely, difficulties and dangers are at once added to the commander's responsibilities. The enemy, being undefeated, spends his time sniping into camp, picking off and stalking sentries, and his attentions are always seriously turned to the water supply. In many cases the river or water supply of a large town is situated half a mile or a mile from its outskirts (in Benin city it is nearly two miles), and water parties, therefore, have to be strongly composed of fighting men, whose duty it is to thoroughly clear the road of the enemy, and protect the carriers while the various vessels are being filled. These water parties are never without their casualties, if the enemy be bold and courageous.

With the "clearing volley" system, and the tactics of remaining on the path and firing into the bush, it is rarely possible to inflict severe losses on the enemy. Sometimes after a volley the boom of a musket is heard some distance in front—an extra nervous man has let off his gun as the bullets from the volley begin to chip the branches over his head, thus "giving away" the ambush, and the enemy retires to his next position without firing a shot. At others, as before depicted, the troops walk into the trap ; but as they expend their ammunition by firing into stockades or earthen parapets, the enemy suffers comparatively little harm, and even should he eventually retire, it is not because he has suffered severe loss. His concealed position has been exposed to view owing to the screen having been cut away, so he thinks he had better be going.

The human animal having carefully concealed himself for the furtherance of his plans, becomes nervous and uncertain, as a rule, should his devices be laid bare. The same savages have been known to evacuate concealed trenches immediately they have become exposed, and still, later on, have stood up and fought well in the open.

Present Methods. Individual Action. The present system of bush fighting is almost diametrically the opposite of that which I have just endeavoured to describe. Then, the bush path was seldom or never left; now, directly fighting begins, troops move into the bush. Then it was all volleys; now individual fire is taught. It means a more highly trained soldier, and one possessing a fire discipline unknown fifteen, perhaps ten, years ago. It is wonderful how soon a native soldier learns to appreciate the trust and responsibility imposed on him by allowing him to fire when he considers it necessary—he is out of sight in the bush; there is no direct influence of his section commander, for, when scouting, he has to rely on himself. He knows he must not let off his rifle at nothing; he also knows he may fire at once if he thinks he can see anything moving in the bush about him. He must remember where the bush path is, and that the other scouts are in line with him; and then the great knowledge comes to him that on his individual effort, on his sense, alertness, and steadiness, depend the safety of his comrades, and perhaps the success of the day. Compare the feelings, behaviour, and *moral* of this man with the soldier who has been taught to fire volleys into space, who never sees one of the enemy, and who has learnt that, as long as he is cool enough to load, aim his carbine about three feet from the ground, and fire when ordered to, nothing else is required of him. The practice of treating the native soldier

TACTICS

like a machine, as if he were devoid of intelligence, is happily a thing of the past. The more the individual is brought out in a man, the more he is trained to think and use his common sense, the better will he be, provided discipline does not suffer.

A peculiar case of individual action took place in the Aro Expedition. An exceedingly indifferent shot belonging to the Southern Nigeria Regiment was on sentry, after the taking of Arochuku. The orderly officer, on going his rounds, could not find this man anywhere, and came in and reported that he must have gone over to the enemy. A short time afterwards he came back to his group, and was at once put under charge of the guard. His excuse for deserting his post was that he saw one of the enemy crawling up through the bush to shoot him, and knowing that it would be useless to fire, as he was such a bad shot, he decided to kill him with his bayonet. Crawling out, therefore, into the bush, he so effectually stalked his man that he was able to accomplish his purpose. His story was not believed until he showed the spot where the dead native lay; and there, sure enough, he was found with a bayonet thrust in the back. So silent had he been, and so thoroughly had he done the job, that none of the other sentries had heard anything.

It is not intended to throw discredit, by criticism, on the tactics and methods of fighting carried out by all the pioneers of West Africa; the tactics they pursued may have been suited to their time and to the tactics of the tribes they had to contend against, but their methods will not do for the present day. We have for several decades been training the natives of Africa to fight, and if, with all our time-expired old soldiers scattered throughout the length and breadth of the land, the tribes had not become better fighting men, and more cunning in the art of war, it would indeed be a poor reflection on our teaching. It behoves us, therefore, to go one better in order to defeat these more highly trained savages.

<small>Savages More Highly Trained Now.</small>

During the Aro campaign in 1901-2, at the fight of Okoroji's Farm, the most elaborate series of beautifully made and concealed trenches was discovered. For about half a mile before the trenches were encountered the country was fairly open, being covered with tufts of grass a few feet high, and stunted bushes. On entering this open country the leading company had reinforced the scouts, and advanced in extended order, followed by the leading maxims and a 75 millimetre gun, ready for action. The flankers were well thrown out. The advance was continued in this formation. When the extended company arrived at a point about 300 yards from where the path and the enemy's trench met (see plan), an exceedingly heavy fire was opened by the enemy. They were well armed, and the Snider bullets began to hum over the heads of the troops, sounding like a swarm of bees. The puffs of smoke of the guns appeared along such a regular line in the bush that trenches and a prepared position were suggested at once. This being so, a halt was made, and, with the object of occupying his attention, the guns opened a heavy fire, directed at the white puffs immediately in front. Parties were then sent right and left to outflank the trenches. The left hand party found none, but seriously interfered with one line of retreat which the enemy had prepared for himself. The right hand party was taken in flank while advancing, and had to turn right hand and charge the enfilading trench, which it did with great dash; then working on, it suc-

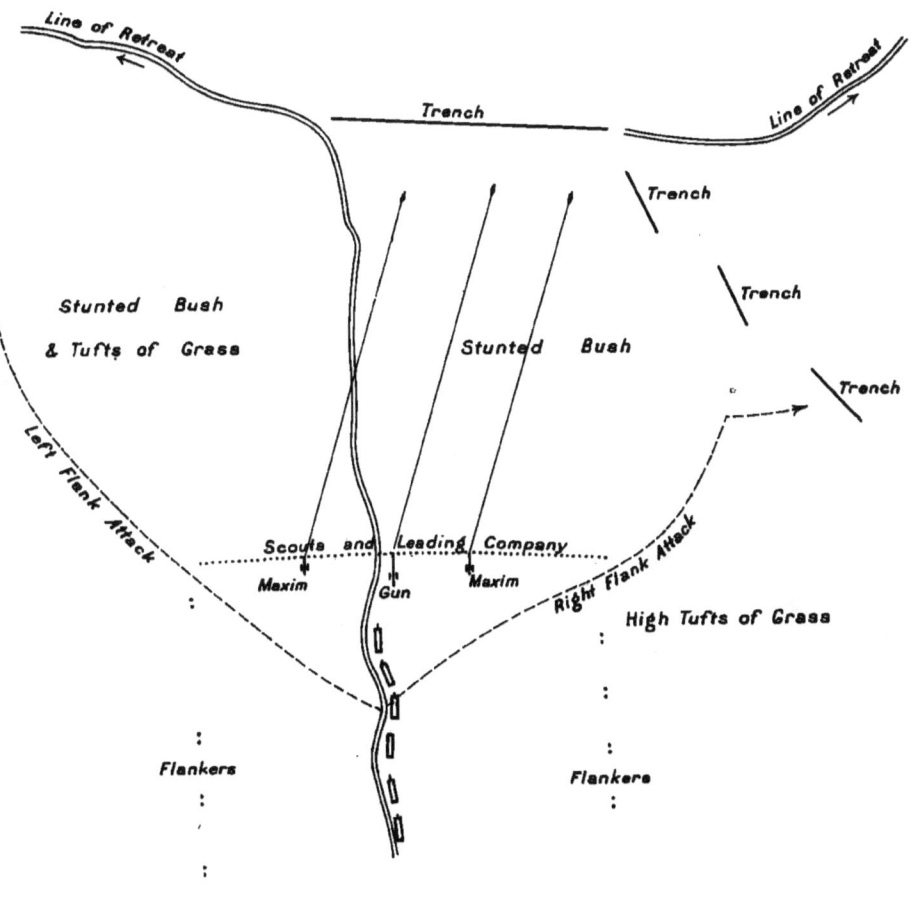

TACTICS

cessively took the remaining trenches, and got on to the enemy's other line of retreat. The guns in the centre then ceased fire, and the trenches in front were taken by assault, thus co-operating with the flanking parties. The enemy fled headlong, and suffered severely. Prisoners afterwards reported that these trenches were manned by 2,500 Aros, and 5,000 more were in the town half a mile off, with swords and matchets, ready to aid in cutting up the column as soon as it had been thrown into confusion. The section and finish of these trenches were admirable, and their well-planned position made it difficult to believe that they were not the work of some highly trained men. It can be seen that this position would not have been taken if the troops had remained on the path and been content to fire volleys at the smoke of the enemy's guns.

Again, in Sir J. Willcocks' book " From Kabul to Kumassi," he speaks of the elaborate stockades made by the Ashantis in 1900. The Kintampo stockade near Kumassi is minutely described, and shows what a formidable work it was. He says: " It was a well designed work about three hundred yards in length; the general alignment was fixed by selecting trees, which formed angles of defence, affording excellent cross fire, and between them timbers of some two or three feet in diameter were placed upright, six feet above and two and a half feet under ground; of these there was a double row, five or six feet apart, and the interior was filled with green trunks, earth and stones, all well rammed down. At every few feet apart there were loopholes. The tops of the timber uprights were bound together with telegraph wire, and there were wire entanglements and concealed pits in the jungle to the front. The ground was well selected, and the

Savage Stockades.

entire work constructed from behind, with a twenty foot clear space in front, beyond which was dense undergrowth."

In speaking of the fight which finally relieved Kumassi, and in which the Ashantis were outmanœuvred and defeated, he speaks of their chief defences being on the main road " by which alone they believed we should advance, and in that direction they had really strong stockades flanked and reflanked by others."

How well they learnt the lesson taught them by Major Baden-Powell in 1896.

The stockades encountered in the Timini country during the Sierra Leone rising in 1898 were formidable structures. Captain Wallis describes them in his book on the subject.

"The logs used for making the stockades were about nine feet long and from fourteen to eighteen inches in diameter. Three feet of their length was buried in the ground, leaving some six feet above, and they were firmly bound together. Huge boulders were then built up against them, and thus a solid stone wall some three to four feet thick was formed; a trench in rear for the firing party, who aimed through hollowed out pieces of banana stalk or bamboo placed in a row close to the ground, completed the work, which was situated close to the path in the densest bush."

Colonel Marshall in his despatch on these operations says :—" It is absolutely impossible for European eyes to discern them by any outward sign; occasionally an exceptionally quick-sighted native will discover the locality of a stockade by some indication, such as a dead twig or some drooping leaves overhead. The places mostly chosen are the crossings of fords and rivers, thick gullies, a sharp turn in the road, the top or bottom of a hill, so long

TACTICS

as it commands the path, and the densest bush in the vicinity of their towns. They are often built in groups giving mutual support. The shells of the 7-pounder break to pieces on coming in contact with these boulders. A sheltered line of retreat down some small slope leading to a pathway cut in rear enables the defenders to retreat in comparative safety. Owing to the density of the bush it is impossible to rush them."

Such things as these elaborate trenches and stockades were at one time unknown, but now tha they are a part of bush warfare, it behoves us, as I say, to put a little more thought and science into our methods and tactics, and not rely altogether on luck and a superior weapon.

It is undoubtedly a difficult matter to protect the long drawn out columns, which are inevitable in bush fighting, from surprise and attack. In the open it is easy enough. Advanced, flank, and rear guards, composed, in some cases in Northern Nigeria, of Mounted Infantry, with their scouts, form adequate screens, but this is impossible in dense or even light bush. It is, again, useless sending an advanced guard some distance on in front, as is done in the open. Any party sent on, and separated more than 100 yards from the main column, unless it is strong enough to look after itself, runs a risk of being surrounded and wiped out. One of the first rules which is impressed on a soldier is that there must be no gaps in the column itself. If desirable, and the force is too large and unwieldy for a single column, it is wise to divide it up into two, and let each march distinct from the other. Let each have sufficient fighting men to make it independent, but never allow gaps to occur between the various portions or groups composing it.

Vulnerable Carrier Column.

Present Method of Scouts and Flankers. In bush countries, and against natives armed with, for the most part, dane guns, but having a percentage of accurate breech-loading rifles, and possessing muzzle-loading cannon, the methods of scouts and flankers have been found advantageous. The scouting is carried out by the leading section, which can be relieved from time to time by a fresh one; or it may be entrusted to a picked body of men, formed into a corps of scouts. It is undoubtedly a good thing in every battalion to have such a corps, composed of a certain number of strong, active men of approved courage; they should be good shots, and should be extra intelligent; they should be granted extra privileges and higher pay. It should be an exceeding honour to be appointed to the corps of scouts, and a corresponding degradation to be relegated to the status of an ordinary soldier. The main body of the scouts advances from 50 to 100 yards ahead of the advanced guard. It throws out so many pairs of scouts to the right, and so many to the left of the path. From 50 to 60 yards in fairly open bush, and much nearer in dense bush, is far enough to have the outermost scouts on each flank. Their pace and movements can be regulated by the whistle, and by the voice of the officer or N.C.O. directing the scouting. Bird-calls are practised in some regiments, and these being used, supersede the voice and whistle as a means of directing movements. They have the advantage of being more in harmony with the noises of the bush, and when done well are most successful.

Care must be exercised that the "point" does not get ahead of the scouts. More pairs than two on each flank may, of course, be thrown out if it is considered necessary, but the smaller the number of men subjected to this trying work, the better. It is naturally only to locate the enemy and his stockades that scouts are used, and as these works are never very far from the path, four scouts in pairs on each flank are, as a rule, enough to disclose the ambush. The scouts should be relieved every ten minutes at most; the heat is intense when working through bush, sometimes with the aid of a matchet, and this, combined with the strain on the man's nerves, soon saps his energy. It is obvious that men working in pairs are more reliable than single scouts. Each man gives the other confidence, and they can help each other should they fall into a trap. Flankers, in the same way, should be thrown out into the bush on each side of the column from all bodies of troops. There are various ways of doing this, and the drill is varied, but a very simple method is as follows:—" Flankers out" being ordered, four men from the head of each separate body of troops in the column are thrown out as flankers, one pair to the right and one to the left, from twenty to thirty yards into the bush, depending on circumstances, their section commander keeping them in touch with the column, and level with himself, by voice. On being relieved they fall in in rear of their section, and a fresh lot go out. By "separate bodies" is meant gun escorts, hospital escorts, companies marching intact, and the various sections or subsections which are distributed throughout the carrier column. It is wonderful how silently a column can move through the bush, although the commanders of the scouts and various section commanders are from time to time directing their men by voice or bird-call. A man's name called in a low tone, just sufficiently loud to reach him, his answering grunt, then the direction, "Come in," "Go more slowly," "Go right," or "Go left," with again his guttural answer, is heard only really a few yards away. Some commanders like to put out two pairs of flankers instead of one, on each flank, and doubtless this would be a wise precaution in certain situations, but it is tiring work. There is a great relief to all on the path in this "scout and flanker" method of advancing, compared with the procedure which was often adopted not very long ago, and which entailed a heavy mental strain on all, officers, soldiers, and carriers alike. At any moment the roar of guns on all sides was usually the first intimation given that the enemy was near. A column now advances with its feelers out on all sides, and only those actually in the bush are subjected to any strain at all, and then only for a short time until relieved. This feeling of safety adds greatly to the efficiency of the troops. Should the ground be open, and it be advisable, all the troops guarding the carriers may march in file on each flank, thus forming a stronger screen than the mere flankers. A body, however, ought to be kept in hand on the path ready to conform to the Commander's wishes.

Directly a halt is made, even for a short time, sentries should be sent out into the bush on all sides to guard against the wily savage, who is always on the look-out for a chance of crawling up and picking off some one at a range of a few yards. These sentries should hide and remain motionless, ready for instant action. After a few of the enemy's stalkers have been badly wounded, their friends will become very chary of adopting this form of warfare.

To sum up the above remarks in a few words: Adopt the tactics of the enemy, train the soldiers to stalk and creep through the bush, and hide behind trees. The savages fear the soldier who can go into the bush after them; they know that once

TACTICS

off the path, the soldier has the advantage. He can shoot quicker and straighter, and an annoying thing is that ordinary trees and brushwood are no protection against his ·303 bullet.

Attached to the scouts it is useful at times to have some expert tree climbers. Natives can be found who without any ropes or aids are able to walk straight up to the top of a cocoa-nut tree sixty feet high. It is a matter of a few seconds only. They grasp the tree with their hands, then with knees slightly bent and toes holding on to the rough surface, simply move up the tree without any apparent effort. They carry a matchet or long knife in their teeth, in case a snake is encountered in the bushy top. Tree Climbers.

These men can look over a country which is not too densely wooded, and can point out towns, and occasionally disclose ambuscades.

Three of them were most useful in the Ubium Expedition of 1900 in Southern Nigeria.

One was employed with No. 4 Column Aro Field Force, and undoubtedly saved the column much trouble and many casualties at the fight at Okoroji's Farm.

That day batches of the Aros had been driven back step by step since early morning by the scouts and advanced sections. At 11.30 a.m., the country being fairly open, the road dropped down to a stream and rose again on the far side, the force halted for breakfast near the water, having the heights crowned all round. The tree climber was sent up the highest tree, and at once reported large bodies of the enemy moving about at the edge of some thin bush about three-quarters of a mile across an open plain to the front. The 75-millimetre and 7-pounder guns with the column opened with indirect fire, direction being given by the man in the tree, who also described the result of each shot. After about the third shot he gave a piercing yell, three up both arms, lost his balance, and it looked as if all was over with him. Like a monkey, however, he clutched a branch in falling and saved himself, then, quite unperturbed, announced with shouts of excitement that the last shot had gone into the middle of the enemy. The artillery preparation proceeded while the force breakfasted, and it was learnt afterwards that the Aro forces suffered a good deal, and were thrown into confusion by the adoption of this device.

Shot Guns. It might be as well here to mention the fact that certain men have advocated the arming of the men of the W.A.F.F. with shot guns, in preference to carbines, for service in thick bush. It is obvious, I think, to all who have done much West African fighting that this policy would be fatal. It would put the enemy on the same footing, as regards his weapon, as our own men, and limit our power of inflicting injury to a comparatively few yards.

Examples of Successful Tactics. Let us suppose now that the scouts have located the enemy behind stockades, and have either fallen back or been reinforced. The enemy's attention should now be occupied while companies or sections are deployed, and dispositions made for taking the stockade in flank and rear; examples taken from two or three campaigns will show what tactics have been successful, and as each method was crowned with success, they are worthy of note. It is manifestly impossible to lay down any precise rules by which an enemy may be defeated, and for this reason I have chosen the following examples for quotation and instruction, instead of endeavouring to lay down the procedure which in various situations might be adopted.

TACTICS

ASHANTI CAMPAIGN, 1900.—Taking of the Pekki Stockade.*

Sir James Willcocks' force consisted of two 75-millimetre Q.F. guns, four 7-pounder guns and six maxims, 60 Europeans, 1,000 native troops, and 1,700 carriers with stores for the beleaguered garrison of Kumassi. On the 15th July, about a quarter past four in the afternoon, the scouts located the stockade which was built across the Pekki road, and which was defended by several thousand Ashantis. No trace of it could be seen by the advanced guard. Small trees and light brushwood had been cut and cleared away on the right, showing that the enemy were also in that direction. The advanced guard no sooner appeared, than the Ashantis opened fire with every weapon they possessed. Major Melliss, in charge of the scouts, Lieutenant Edwards and several men were wounded almost at once.

Lieut.-Col. Wilkinson, in command of the advanced guard, had been ordered to concentrate all his artillery as well as his maxims, and with these to open a heavy fire on the enemy with the object of making him keep under cover, while the force extended and enveloped his flank. Accordingly, the two quick firing guns were brought up on the road; to the right of these was placed one 7-pounder, and still further to the right and facing the newly cut bush, were the two other 7-pounders. The advanced guard maxims also came up into line, and all these guns swept the bush with a tornado of lead. The Ashantis kept up an equally heavy return fire, but one of their number confessed afterwards that the fire from the guns was so heavy and accurate that they dared not raise themselves

*From Kabul to Kumassi, by Sir J. Willcocks, K.C.M.G.

high enough to fire over the stockade, which was not loopholed, and consequently their shooting was high. It would have been impossible for the gunners to have existed, and for the infantry to have extended where they did, had it not been for this.

Sir J. Willcocks' object, as he says in his account of the fight, was "to extend all the troops of the advanced guard and main body under cover of our shell and maxim fire, leaving the carriers temporarily to the charge of the rear guard, and as soon as this was attained, to order a general bayonet charge." The guns were well commanded by Lieut. Phillips, and each shell either went into the stockades or just over them. The infantry in the meantime were extending, until the line of bayonets was over five hundred yards in length, the right well thrown back and parallel to the alignment of the enemy's defences and war camps. The supreme moment had now arrived. The guns poured in the heaviest possible fire for a minute, then the massed buglers were ordered to sound the "cease fire"; as the notes rang out, the order was implicitly obeyed, and the dead silence which ensued strangely affected the Ashantis, who also ceased fire. The bugles then took up the "charge," and, headed by their officers, the black troops swept over the stockades and drove the enemy in headlong flight. The "assembly" then sounded. Scouts were thrown out on all sides, and the advance in to Kumassi was made.

This is an example of a frontal attack carried out with success.

IBEKU-OLOKORO EXPEDITION.—Fight outside the town of Onor.

The force consisted of one 75-millimetre gun, 2

maxims, 12 Europeans, 226 rank and file, and 232 carriers. The 226 men were composed of nine sections taken from various garrisons in the Aro country.

The advanced guard, commanded by Captain Grayson, R.A., which was the fighting portion of this small force, consisted of scouts, 3½ sections infantry, one 75-millimetre gun, and 1 maxim, or about 90 men. The scouts were under Lieutenant Macdonnell, D.S.O., an excellent officer of the permanent forces of Canada. Half a mile out of the friendly town of Onor the road ran along a narrow causeway, about 100 yards in length, and with a deep swamp on either side; there was a small stream at the enemy's end of it which had to be waded. Fire was opened on the scouts, the enemy disputing the passage of the stream from the opposite bank. The scouts kept the enemy employed while the 75-millimetre and maxim were got into position. A heavy fire was then poured in, and before the enemy had recovered, the guns ceased fire and a section of the advanced guard dashed across, and extended out in the open yam fields beyond. The enemy retired precipitately, having only been holding the water with scouts.

The path now ran up the face of a hill covered with plantations, and became a hollow road, with sides 15 to 20 feet high near the brow. A strong stockade closed the hollow road, and the scouts reported trenches on each side of it, filled with the enemy, just over the crest of the hill. Captain Grayson engaged the attention of the enemy in front, while he sent Lieut. Macdonnell with the bulk of the advanced guard round the enemy's left through the plantations; these afforded very fair cover, but were easy to move through. Lieut. Macdonnell went well round, but was confronted by new trenches.

He was able to creep up close to these unseen, owing to their being placed too far back from the crest of the hill. He cleared them with the bayonet, and cut the enemy's line of retreat, who, being now pressed in front, evacuated his trenches and fled into the bush.

ASHANTI EXPEDITION, 1873.*

Colonel Wolseley had three British battalions, a small Naval brigade, as well as certain native levies and a detachment of the 2/ W.I. Regiment for this campaign. The advance of the main column was direct on Kumassi through the towns of Amoaful and Ordahsu. The fight at Amoaful is described by Lord Wolesley, and gives an idea of the tactics :
" My little army breakfasted early, and moved off at daybreak on January 31st, 1874, all ranks feeling they had a tough job before them that day. I was convinced we should be attacked in flank and rear by the enemy, as their immense superiority in numbers would enable them to carry out to the fullest extent their favourite tactics of surrounding the army opposed to them, and my force was too small to prevent it. I determined, therefore, to advance in what I may describe as a large open square formation, each side having its own selected commander. The position to be occupied by each battalion was carefully explained to each commanding officer. The front fighting line was to be between six and seven hundred yards in width, its centre being marked by Rait's guns on or near the Kumassi Road. The rockets were to be at the front angles of the parallelogram. The troops on the side faces were to cut paths as they pushed

*The Story of a Soldier's Life, by Lord Wolesley.

orward through the underscrub, each at a distance of about 300 yards from the road. My force was too small to enable me to prevent the enemy from getting all round us, and he had also the great advantage of being able to move easily through the dense forest, where we could only pass by cutting paths, a slow, difficult, and dangerous operations."

"Two miles along a bad path took me to a few little huts, which constituted the village of Quarman. The day's work began about 9 a.m. with some desultory firing in the vicinity of a small village called Eganassee, a couple of miles beyond Quarman. Lord Gifford with his scouts drove the enemy out with little difficulty, but sent back to say the Ashantis were in considerable force beyond the village. In cutting the paths for the side faces of the square, poor Capt. Buckle, of the R.E., was killed early in the day. . . . .

"As soon as we began to move forward it became apparent that the enemy meant to make a determined resistance. . . . .

"The fight soon raged loudly on all sides. It was a curious sensation, that of being fired into upon four faces of our big square by a howling mass of many many thousands of savages determined to kill us or die in the attempt, and yet to be unable to see them in the dense bush beneath that awe-inspiring forest."

For some little time not much progress was made, the Ashantis attacking vigorously, and the sides in some instances being hard pressed and requiring reinforcements.

"The enemy fought well under the terrific fire we poured into them, and had they been armed with Snider rifles we must have been destroyed. As they fell back, bit by bit, the spirits of our men rose, and a British cheer at times told one things were looking brighter all round. On coming to a village clearance I would not allow the houses to be loopholed, lest such a defensive precaution might cause any weak-hearted men to doubt, even for a moment, that success, complete success, was not a certainty. [Showing Lord Wolseley's appreciation of the fact that only by advancing, attacking and pressing the enemy, victory could be ensured.] The front line was commanded by Brigadier-General Sir A. Alison, whose objective was the village of Amoaful. It was taken at noon by a well-directed charge of the Black Watch, and I was glad to learn at the same time that it was large enough to afford cover for my little army with all its wounded."

The enemy now drew off, having had enough, and although the lines of communication were subject to repeated attacks, the head of the army was not molested for the remainder of the day. Amoaful was placed in a state of defence and turned into an advanced depot. On the 2nd February the advance was resumed, but was not seriously opposed at first; the Ordah River was crossed on February 4th, and the final fights and advance into Kumassi made the same day.

During the day's fighting the bravery and fierceness with which the Ashantis attacked while the column was on the pure defensive, and the utter collapse and rout which accompanied a renewal of the advance when the Black Watch began their six mile rush which opened the road into Kumassi, are peculiarly striking.

"At 9 a.m., after about two unpleasant hours of hard fighting and slow progress, the village of Ordahsu was in our possession, though the enemy, defiant as ever, still surrounded it on three sides. All our reserve stores of every nature were now

TACTICS

quickly and safely passed through the double line of troops I had formed between the river and the village. The enemy held in force some ravines which came down from the upper level to the river, and from them they made fierce onslaughts upon what I may call my 'covered way' between the bridge and the village."

From now until noon, during which time the stores were being transferred to the village, no advance took place, and the Ashantis appeared to have redoubled their efforts and to have imagined that they might be able to overcome the white man.

"A little after 11 a.m., I transferred my headquarters from the bridge to the village. For an hour after I had entered it the place was a regular 'inferno.' Rait's guns in action, a deafening roar of musketry on all sides, and the loud banging of the enemy's muskets, fired as fast as they could load them, all round the outside of the place."

The Black Watch then began their advance, and were for the first moment, as they pushed forward from Ordahsu, met with a terrific fire; many fell wounded, but nothing could stop them. The Ashantis seemed at last to realize this, for the shouting in front ceased for a moment as they fled in all directions in wild confusion."

No quiescent action, therefore, when in touch with the enemy can ever hope to succeed. The purely defensive in war has never been successful.

Although in this campaign tactics were adopted which are different in detail from those in vogue at the present day, still, the main idea was the same, viz., attack.

The square steadily advanced and did not remain in one position in order to ply the enemy with fire. The gradual advance drove the Ashantis back and prevented them from taking up positions from which they could lie for an hour or more in comparative safety and fire their guns as fast as their three or four loaders could ram home charges. This gradual advance in time broke the spirit of the boldest of the enemy—and they certainly did not lack as far as bravery was concerned—and paved the way for the final advance and charge of the 42nd Highlanders, which drove the Ashantis headlong and finished the campaign.

BENIN EXPEDITION, 1897.

In the campaign for the capture of Benin City in 1897, the Binis relied nearly altogether on ambuscades and dane-gun fire from the dense bush to repel the invaders. The road was only barred by a stockade in one place, and that was a crude affair.

Admiral Rawson's main column was composed of an advanced fighting portion, while a supporting one followed it.

Colonel Bruce Hamilton commanded the fighting portion. It was under 500 of all ranks, and consisted of 50 scouts, 4 companies of native troops, 100 marines, two 7-pounder guns, two maxims, and a rocket tube. The camp at Ologbo was attacked with determination, but the enemy were driven off without many casualties to the troops. Once the advance began through the thick bush, in the direction of Benin City, the Binis fought with great bravery and determination.

It was found that they had cut an ambush path parallel to the regular bush path, and some ten yards from it. This was found most useful, for, by sending a detachment along it, a broader front for the advance was possible. The advance was conducted by the scouts firing occasional clearing volleys.

TACTICS

Commander Bacon in his book, "Benin, The City of Blood," says: "Steadily and slowly we marched, occasionally hearing signal guns fired by the Binis, till at last at 10 a.m. the scouts reported the enemy in force ahead. As the scouts had none too much ammunition and were only raw levies, Colonel Hamilton opened them out, and took the leading company of Hausas, maxim and rocket tube through them, and having found the ambush path, Captain Carter took his men along that. We then passed from the monotony of the march to the excitement of a running fight, firing sectional volleys and then advancing; the enemy yelling and firing, then retiring and again advancing with a yell." And so it went on. The Binis endeavoured to ambush the columns, but the clearing volleys always disclosed the trap, and as there were no stockades and trenches, at least none such as the tribes have since learnt to construct, the steady advance and volleys gradually drove back the King of Benin's army and bore down all opposition. A description of one stockade is given; it was built across the path so that there was no attempt at ambush or concealment. It seems to have been erected in a strong place, and had it been held by some warlike tribes having war experience, the taking of it might have been a serious matter. The Binis, however, although of undoubted bravery, had no experience. Commander Bacon thus describes it: "We next met a stockade erected between two high banks through which the path ran. In front was a causeway over a ravine about twenty feet deep; in the stockade could be seen a gun. Volleys from the bank seemed to clear the stockade, and the maxim was set to work at it while the 7-pounder came up. A common shell was fired, but did no damage, so the demolition party were called upon to blow it up. This was easy, as the maxim and 7-pounder had caused all the Binis to quit. 16¼ lbs. of gun cotton in a canvas hose placed at the base blew it literally to smithereens." The Binis had suffered severely up to this, or the task at the stockade would not have been so simple. They made one more determined stand, however, at the entrance to Benin City, but once the city was taken, there seemed to be a 'sauve qui peut,' for not a single gun was fired again at the white man, and the troops and carriers could even go to the water, 1¾ miles off, without danger of being sniped at. This utter collapse of the Binis, after fighting so well, has always been a matter of surprise, and shows conclusively that they must have sustained very heavy losses while endeavouring to drive back the invaders. Although they did not hold carefully concealed trenches and stockades, as the tribes have now learnt to do, still they must have stood up in great numbers, simply relying on their guns, and so have sustained heavy losses. The massacre of the peaceful expedition some six weeks before had evidently given them confidence in their powers and ability to destroy the white man and his soldiers without much trouble.

Taking of the Stockade near Karsi by the Lagos Column, under Captain Aplin.—Ashanti, 1900.

One 7-pounder gun, 2 maxims, 6 Europeans, and 250 native soldiers composed the column. Soon after leaving Karsi, about three miles from Kumassi, the rear guard was attacked, and the firing became general all up the length of the column in a very short space of time. The bush on both sides of

TACTICS

the path swarmed with the enemy, while a great many had taken up positions in trees, and poured a heavy fire on to the troops, who did not enter the bush, but volleyed right and left from the path.

Only a very slow advance was possible, and not much more than a mile was covered in five hours.

The situation appeared hopeless, when quite suddenly the enemy seemed to draw off, and at once a more rapid advance was resorted to. Before, however, they had gone far, a formidable stockade was found blocking the road round a sharp bend.

The enemy had retired behind this, and now swept the path with a concentrated fire. A maxim and the 7-pounder were brought up, but the detachments were shot down so quickly that their fire was soon silenced. The rear guard was now called upon to send up reinforcements, and Captain Read and thirty of these men made a gallant charge, and arrived within a few yards of the stockade. He could get no further, however, for most of his men had been shot, and being himself wounded in five places, and practically alone, he was compelled to retire to shelter round the bend of the road.

Matters were now desperate.

The maxims had jammed, while the 7-pounder ammunition ran short, and gravel and stones were used as projectiles for the remaining charges of powder.

Captain Aplin now decided to carry out a manœuvre which, had it been tried at first, might have shortened the fight considerably.

A party of 25 Hausas, under Captain Cochrane, who gallantly volunteered his services, although suffering from a severe wound in the shoulder, was told off to carry out a flank attack.

Taking advantage of a narrow path which led

away into the bush, the party managed to get, unseen, to within a few yards of the stockade, and poured several volleys into the surprised Ashantis. which, followed at once by a charge front and flank, succeeded in taking the stockade. The enemy fled in all directions into the bush.

The day's fight resulted in 2 men being killed, 4 officers and 122 men being wounded, or nearly 50 per cent. of the force.

The above is especially of interest, as it was a mixture of the old and new tactics. As soon as the troops left the path and entered the bush, victory crowned their efforts.

The above few examples are sufficient to show the tactics which have been successful against an enemy who fights in open bush, and also against one who has learnt to build formidable stockades, and knows how to defend them.

Lieut. Wright, V.C.

While on the subject of what has been done, and what can be done, against savages in the bush, Lieutenant Wright's brilliant feat of arms during the Kano-Sokoto campaign should not be overlooked. This officer was in command of 44 native mounted infantry, and had been sent out to the flank of General Kemball's force advancing on Sokoto, to patrol the country and reconnoitre.

Two days out he fell in with a large party of the enemy, whom he promptly charged and dispersed.

The next day the Kano army attacked him, led by the Waziri of that town. It consisted of some 1,200 horse and 2,000 foot.

Lieut. Wright kept to the thickest bush he could find, made a zareba of thorns, and placed his carbines at intervals of three paces round the perimeter. His carriers, prisoners, and horses were in the centre. For some two hours the enemy attacked, and charged the little force, but were driven off, and finally retired, leaving some 300 dead and wounded. Amongst the former was the Waziri himself. For Lieutenant Wright's bravery, and fearless example by which he inspired his men, he was awarded the Victoria Cross.

It is exceedingly annoying to a commander when, instead of two or three really decisive engagements, the enemy will not fight, but resorts to the tactics of sniping and cutting off stragglers. These were more or less the tactics of the natives in the two subsequent expeditions for the final subjugation of the Benin country. The first of these was against Ologbo Shiri, the head war chief of the King of Benin. He had collected a large following and taken up his stronghold in the country east of Benin City, and from there defied the Government. Major C. H. P. Carter, Royal Scots, was sent against him with a force. His people had evidently learnt to a great extent the danger of resisting the white man in the way they had when defending Benin City, and although they made a good fight the first day the expedition advanced against Ologbo Shiri's stronghold, still, they did not wait long enough to suffer severely, but confined themselves to sniping the camps and in laying wait for any force which moved out. They succeeded with one or two of their ambuscades in inflicting some casualties. The country was, however, thoroughly patrolled, and all stores of food either destroyed or brought into the main camp. Various deserters then came in and betrayed the enemy's camps and hiding places in the bush, and these, being at once attacked and rushed, wore the enemy out, and finally resulted in the capture of Ologbo Shiri himself as he and a few of his remaining followers were one day near a village in search of food. The second expedition mentioned above,

Benin Territories Expedition, 1899.

and called the Ishan Expedition, was in the territory of that name, north-east of Benin City.

Ishan Expedition, 1902. The Ishan people had evidently been watching the two previous expeditions in the Benin country with anxiety, and decided that stratagem and cunning were the factors which would aid them in their struggle against the conquerors of Benin City. Their tactics were interesting. The Ishan territories were divided into two parts, the town of Ulia was the head town of the northern section, that of Uromi the stronghold of the southern people. Each district was populous and the natives determined. The southern one was entered first, and the towns on the way to Uromi were found almost deserted, no opposition being met with. In every place one or two people remained to say that the inhabitants did not want to fight, but were anxious to be friends with the white man; also that the King of the country was anxious to be friendly, but that he was a very old man, " even too old to travel in a hammock, so if the white man would only go to Uromi matters could be settled." After endless negotiations the force marched to Uromi and encamped. It is needless to state that every precaution had been observed in the various camps, and especially in this one in the chief town, to guard against surprise, and not without reason. The King could not be seen on arrival, and the people said that word would be sent to him that the white man had arrived. Then without warning the country rose, fiercely attacked two detachments which were visiting outlying towns, and these had to fight their way back to Uromi. The chief of a neighbouring country, with a retinue, on his way to pay his respects, was waylaid, some of his people killed, and he arrived with a few followers in camp more dead than alive, having crawled through the bush.

TACTICS

Another party from another country were massacred, only one man escaping, and he appeared in the camp badly wounded, and related how he had escaped also by hiding in the bush. For a fortnight communications were cut with Benin City, and grave fears for the safety of the expedition were entertained. Perpetual fighting night and day ensued. The whole nation was encamped in the towns round, and their incessant tom-tomming at night showed that orgies and dancing were in progress, celebrating the holding up of the white man. Most of the men massacred were eaten at these feasts, and in one case an unexpected attack on one town interrupted the progress of an entertainment —the troops found a man roasting whole in the market place. Systematic measures had to be adopted. A fighting column left camp every morning, and one after another each town in the country was attacked and taken. All the juju groves were cut down, and stores of food either destroyed or carried back to camp. The enemy was most determined, and nearly every place was vigorously defended. Finally they gave in, the principal men surrendered and were held as hostages for the good behaviour of the people, while the force prepared to enter the northern district, the inhabitants of which, far from being disheartened at the fate which had overtaken their countrymen, breathed defiance, and daily sent insulting messages daring the white man to advance into their country. The change now in the tactics was most marked. A thick belt of bush some four miles wide, without a town or village in it, separated the two districts. What possessed the Ulia people to change their tactics did not transpire, but change they did. Instead of a cunning policy, the opposite course was resorted to, and the whole country turned out into this piece of bush to defend their stronghold. No sooner was the thick bush entered and the boundary line between the two districts crossed, than scouts and flankers were thrown out and almost immediately found the enemy. No stockades or entrenchments had been made, and the enemy fought as their countrymen did on the Ologbo Road, they attacked incessantly front, flanks and rear. A very slow but steady advance was kept up, and whenever the pressure became very severe at a point, a section or so charged into the bush and dislodged the enemy; they were never allowed to go far, 100 yards was quite enough, the enemy flying in all directions. They then returned to their place in the column, and the enemy, not a whit discouraged, collected again at another point along the road and attacked again as vigorously as ever. Ulia was entered about 2 p.m., and with its capture, resistance practically ceased. Some of the towns subsequently acknowledged that 50 per cent. of their fighting men had fallen in the fight.

Different Tactics Required More Inland. The above tactics apply altogether to bush countries. As one proceeds inland and leaves the forest belt, the country gradually gets more open, necessitating different formations and tactics. The inhabitants are also a different class of people—not so well armed as regards firearms, but withal of a more courageous spirit, perhaps, than the forest tribes. They go in more for shock tactics, are armed with bows, poisoned arrows and swords and choose their towns as defensive positions. Some of the largest are surrounded by high walls, built of mud, well puddled, and then dried layer by layer in the sun. Their hardness is such that the 75-millimetre gun is powerless to breach them. The walls of Kano, for example, in Northern Nigeria, are thirteen miles in circumference and

TACTICS

fifty feet high, and quite impervious to gun-fire. The town can only be entered by certain gates, which are well defended by loopholing the walls.

The tactics in Northern Nigeria are necessarily varied, depending on the region and on the tribes to be encountered. In some places mounted infantry can do all the scouting necessary; in other parts horses cannot be used. As a rule, the bush is not thick, and one can generally see fifty or a hundred yards; but in the rains the grass grows to a height of from four to eight feet, and restricts the view. This applies to the centre and south of the Protectorate. In the north the country is very open. The operations might be divided into three classes. *Northern Nigeria Tactics.*

(a) Against savages armed with bows and arrows in close country. (It is only on the borders of Southern Nigeria and Lagos that dane guns are met with.)

(b) Against horsemen and footmen armed with firearms, as well as bows and arrows, in open country.

(c) Against walled and fortified towns.

For (a) the tactics approximate to those which are employed in bush countries.

For (b) square formations are the basis. The squares are formed, as a rule, by men in single rank, and sometimes have to be at one pace interval in order to include the impedimenta; but these squares are not formed until within touch of the enemy.

As Major Callwell, in his "Small Wars," states, there are two kinds of squares—"the rigid form, and the elastic form." The former consists of the shoulder-to-shoulder formation, which we were accustomed to use in the Soudan to resist the fanatical rushes of hordes of Dervishes, and meant more or less a rectangle of four sides, all of which were of nearly equal length.

The men were in touch on the faces, guns were placed at the angles, and the impedimenta were in the centre.

The Ashanti Campaign of 1873 is the sole example of the attempt to employ the rigid form of square in thick bush. The side faces could only advance and keep touch by cutting paths, and the progress was necessarily very slow.

Under the term "elastic square" every other bush formation might be included, from the group organization of General Dodds in Dahomey, detailed elsewhere, to the long-drawn-out columns of our later expeditions, in which the flankers are the side faces of the square, and the fighting portion, or advanced guard, and the rear guard are the front and rear faces respectively. The rigid form is employed in the open in Northern Nigeria.

Bida-Ilorin Expedition, 1906. In the Bida-Ilorin Expedition, the advance against Bida was carried out in the rigid square formation. The country was, for the most part, open, and the enemy relied on the shock tactics of their cavalry, combined with the fire of their foot soldiers, to overthrow the Niger Company's troops.

The force consisted of—
    One 12-pounder Whitworth B.L. gun.
    One 9   „   „   „
    Five 7   „   R.M.L. guns.
    Six maxims. 32 Europeans.
    512 rank and file, and 565 carriers.
Or just over 1,100 personnel.

The infantry were divided into seven companies.

One company formed the front face, one the rear face, while two companies formed each side face of the square. The remaining company was told off to the guns, which had to be dragged by

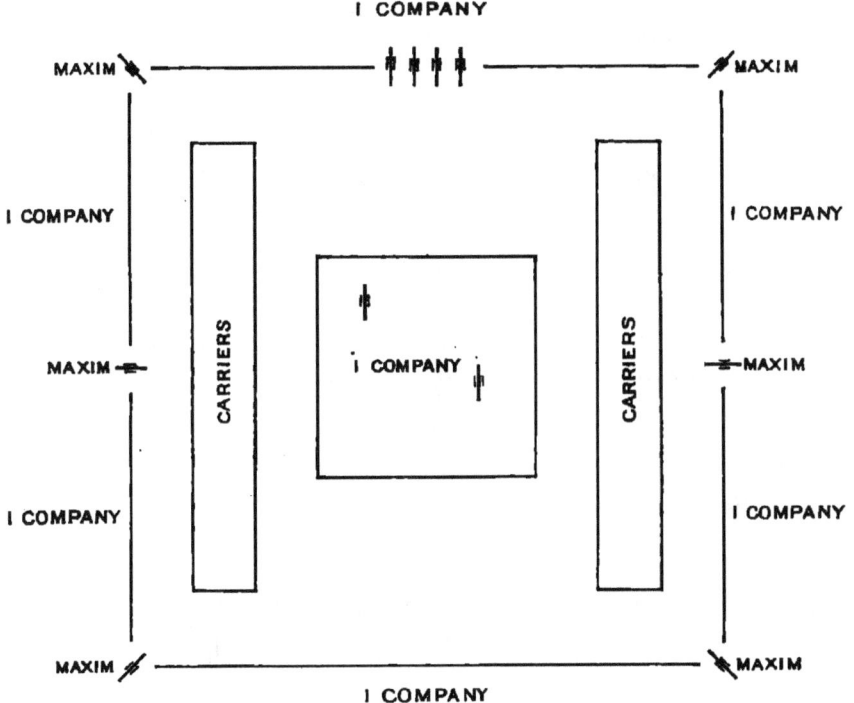

SQUARE FORMATION,
BIDA-ILORIN EXPEDITION, 1896-7.

AFIKPO EXPEDITION, 1902-3.

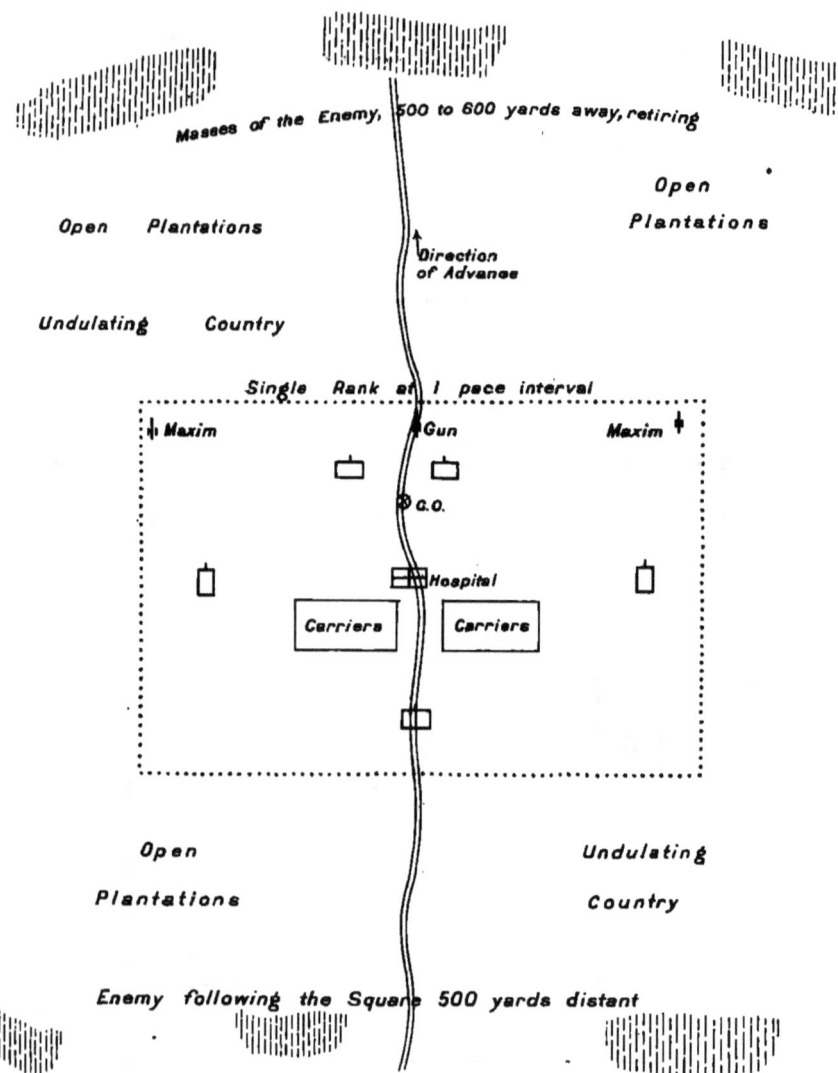

TACTICS

hand, and rendered the advance very slow and tedious.

The guns were in the centre, while the carriers, divided into four bodies, marched two on each side of the square, closed up as much as possible.

During the bombardment of Bida, some of the artillery occupied the centre of the front face.

Overlooking the town of Bida a halt was made and the bombardment was carried out at a range of about 600 yards, and under this the hostile forces soon dispersed.

This was a fight in the open, however, and no dense bush held masses of the enemy or obstructed the view. Still, in terrain of this description, as well as in the thick bush, the only tactics which can hope to succeed are those of an offensive nature.

Sometimes considerable distances have to be traversed in square, and on one occasion in Northern Nigeria a force was moved for four miles in this formation, as the enemy's horsemen were hovering round, and the country gave opportunities to the enemy for lying in ambush.

In Southern Nigeria the Afikpo country is open and undulating. During the expedition (1902-3) against these people, the force advanced some distance in square formation with the carriers in the centre. The bulk of the advanced guard and scouts were extended at one pace interval equally on each side of the main road, which was slightly raised above the surrounding plantations. A 75-millimetre gun was on the road, and at the front angles of the square were maxims. The carriers closed up and marched in a compact body in the centre with a front of thirty to forty yards. The carrier guards and rear guard protected the flanks and rear. Intact bodies of troops were held in readiness in the centre to reinforce any face requiring assistance.

Afikpo Expedition, 1902-3.

As the country was open and the enemy only possessed dane guns, and were not in the habit of charging with swords and spears, they were harmless if kept at a distance of two hundred yards from any face. Thousands of them hovered round the square and watched it from the tops of small hills as a deliberate advance was made against the chief stronghold of the country.

The object of the expedition being not to slaughter the inhabitants but to give them a lesson and to bring them to terms, orders were given that no shot was to be fired except at those of the enemy who came within two hundred yards of any face. Independent fire was used, and very deliberate practise was made. The gun and maxims never came into action during the advance. Individuals and small parties of the enemy endeavoured to get close enough to the square to injure it with their fire, but never lived to get within range of their guns. Had promiscuous firing been resorted to by guns and carbines, masses of the enemy, five and six hundred yards off, would have been mown down, and as a great many of these were merely spectators waiting their chance to join in should the day go against the troops, but equally prepared to give in should their fighting contingent be worsted, it would have been slaughter for no object. The irresistible advance, coupled with the fact that instant death was meted out to all who ventured too near the square, produced an immense impression. The enemy suffered very severely as it was, for they were full of pluck, and the track of the square for some miles was marked by the corpses of their fighting men. Although they attacked continuously from 8.30 a.m. until 12 mid-day, at which hour the town was taken, only one soldier was wounded during the advance in square. A white flag came in that evening. Although these humane tactics might not always do, and in certain cases it would not be safe to let the enemy approach to 200 yards before opening fire, still it was successful in this case, and is an additional example and argument, if one were needed, that methods and tactics should be changed and modified to suit particular cases and people.

The battle of Jidballi, in Somaliland, is a good example of the elastic square used in the open. [margin: Battle of Jidballi, Somaliland.]

Sir Charles Egerton's dispositions* were as follows :—

He left all his baggage, water tins, and other impedimenta in bivouac, under a strong guard, consisting of two sections of mounted infantry, 210 rifles of various corps, and two maxims under command of Major W. B. Mullins, 27th Punjabis. At 5 a.m. the fighting force moved off in double echelon formation (see plan), the front and right flanks being covered by No. 5 Company Somali Mounted Infantry and the Gadabursi Horse, the left flank by the Tribal Horse. At 8.30 a.m. the advanced scouts reported the enemy in force at Jidballi occupying the near edge of a depression in the ground and formed up in a rough semi-circle about $2\frac{1}{2}$ miles in circumference. Lieut.-Col. Kenna was instructed to take the mounted troops, make a wide turning movement, threaten the enemy's right flank and rear, and cut off his retreat. The echelon advanced until within 800 yards of the position, when it halted. The enemy could be seen lying down in the grass and scattered bushes. Heavy firing was now heard from the direction taken by the mounted troops. As the halt was made, the enemy opened an ill-directed fire. The

---

*Despatches of Major General Sir C. Egerton in "London Gazette," Friday, Sept. 2nd, 1904.

guns now came into action and shelled the main zareba, firing also case into some bushes 500 to 600 yards away on the left front. The Hampshires and 27th Punjabis were thrown forward so as to bring their fire to bear on the enemy.

The enemy now began to advance in regular skirmishing order, making short rushes from cover to cover. This attack soon died away, for few of the Dervishes managed to get within 400 yards owing to the severe maxim and rifle fire.

The Somali Mounted Infantry and Gadabursi Horse had got too close to a body of the enemy, by whom they were suddenly rushed while dismounted, and a good deal of confusion occurred. Two determined rushes were now made against the front and right flank, but were met by a terrific fire, and the enemy broke and fled. The pursuit was carried out with great vigour by Col. Kenna, who pursued over some eighteen miles of country. The enemy numbered from 3,000 to 6,000 men, and lost in killed alone 1,200 to 1,500.

Our casualties were 27 killed and 37 wounded all ranks.

Kano-Sokoto, 1903. Again in Northern Nigeria in 1903, in Kano-Sokoto Expedition, commanded by Brigadier-General Kemball, the dispositions at the capture of Sokoto on the 15th March were as follows :—

On the 14th March the force had halted four miles from the city of Sokoto, and a reconnaissance in force had been made in the afternoon with two companies of infantry, 100 M.I., a gun and a maxim. It had been ascertained that the enemy did not intend to fight behind their walls, as they had done at Kano a month earlier, and that it would be unnecessary to prepare for assault of a gate or escalade by means of ladders. It was found that the country round the city was very open, that the enemy's horse was numerous, and that the fighting would take place in the plain outside the walls.

The camp was put in a state of defence, and about 120 men left there with the baggage; the rest of the force, which consisted of about 600 infantry, 100 Mounted Infantry, four guns and four maxims, under Colonel Morland, moved off at daybreak. The advance was made in column of route well closed up, covered by the mounted infantry, until a ridge was reached, one mile from Sokoto, overlooking the city. The enemy were observed issuing from the gates in thousands and forming up outside the walls.

Square was now formed and the British force advanced into the valley, where some difficult ground, cut up by gardens, hedges, and a stream, had to be crossed. Here a few fanatics were encountered, but the square soon reached the edge of the plateau, where it came under the fire of the enemy's sharp-shooters. A halt was made here to drive off the latter, the mounted infantry being thrown out to each flank. The square then advanced, halting from time to time to fire. The effect of shrapnel, maxims and rifles on the enemy's masses was irresistible, and every attempt that they made to charge melted away under the fire concentrated on it. By the time the city was reached all resistance was at an end. Some of the enemy's horsemen made a demonstration against the camp, where the baggage had been left, but encountering a warm reception hurriedly withdrew.

Another party following up the square at a distance was successfully ambushed by a company concealed in a hamlet.

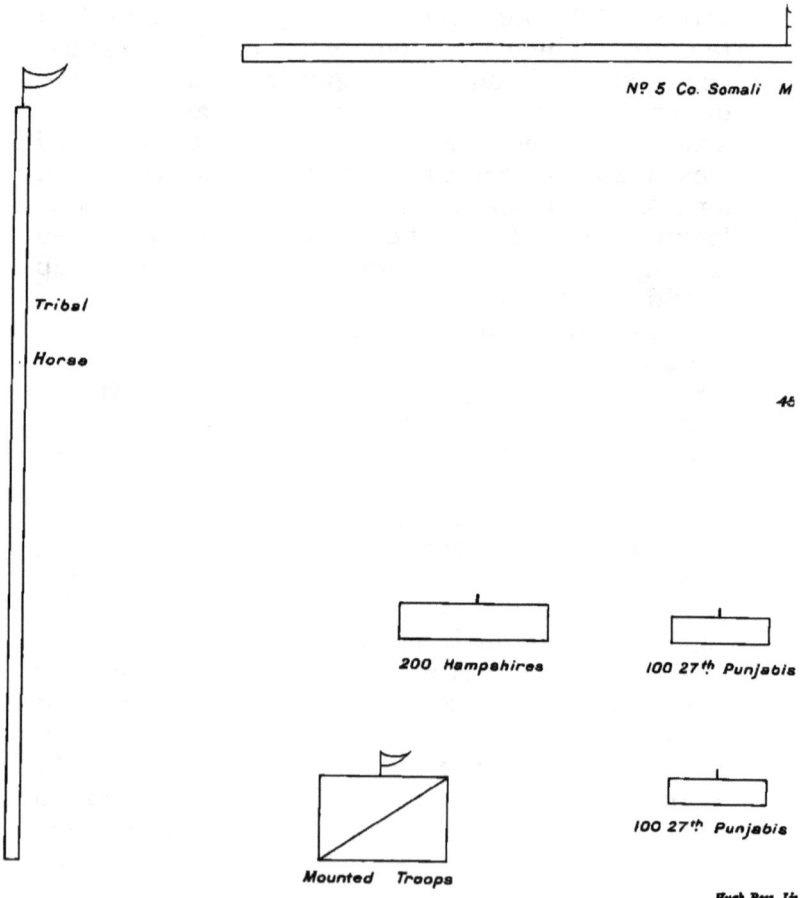

DISPOSITIONS BEFORE
10th Janu[ary]

BATTLE OF JIDBALLI.
ary 1904.

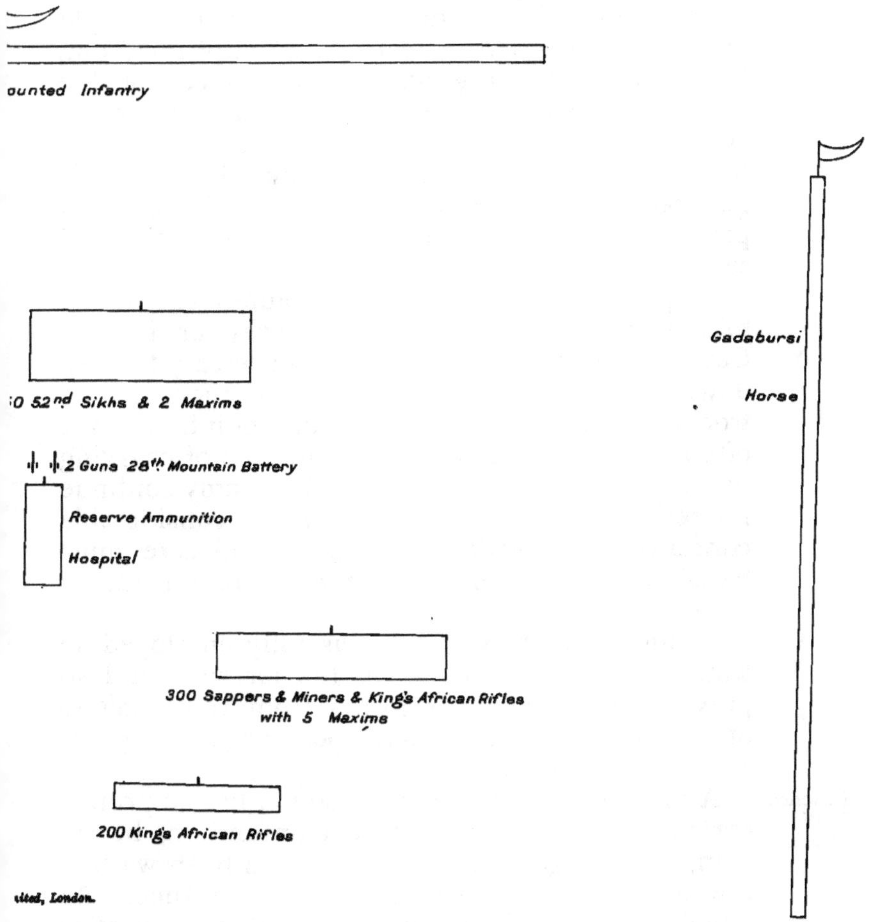

ounted Infantry

52ⁿᵈ Sikhs & 2 Maxims

2 Guns 28ᵗʰ Mountain Battery

Reserve Ammunition

Hospital

300 Sappers & Miners & King's African Rifles with 5 Maxims

200 King's African Rifles

Gadabursi

Horse

Walled Towns. (c) In storming walled towns of any strength, gateways are the best points of attack, and careful reconnaissance is necessary before commencing to breach them with guns, as ammunition is precious, and not easily replaced so far inland.

Sometimes the enemy can be induced to fight outside, and feigned retreats often tempt them out, but they get cunning after having once felt the effects of fire in the open. If the place has to be stormed, it is as well to try and arrange for enfilade fire, but in the case of big cities like Kano this is generally impossible. Feints should be made if possible at different points, as well as at the spot selected for assault.

A special body of troops in column should be told off for the assault of a gateway or breach. Covering fire by troops in line is necessary to keep down the enemy's fire up to the last moment. If troops are moved in line to storm a point, they are often apt to stop and open fire instead of charging into the gap. Street fighting, if the enemy continue his resistance inside, generally causes considerable confusion, and leads to casualties, and care must be taken to stop the fire of the troops outside in time.

Mounted infantry can be usefully employed in watching the main exits on the far side, and so preventing the enemy's forces from retreating to other towns. Important personages may be captured in this manner.

Extended Elastic Square. A force on the move or in action has to protect certain impedimenta, such as ammunition, bearer company, baggage, etc., and often in bush warfare the supplies and provisions for a certain time. As attack may come from any quarter, flanking parties have to be thrown out, and these, together with the advanced and rear guards, form protection on all sides.

TACTICS

The force, therefore, moves in what has been called an "extended elastic square."

In the bush the enemy generally attacks by fire, and does not use shock tactics. It is consequently not necessary to have the shoulder-to-shoulder formations. Parties, sections, and companies may charge away for a short distance, and so increase the gaps in the faces which the elastic formation allows; but, provided the charge is only for a short distance, and that the troops return to their places, no danger need be anticipated from having these breaks in the line.

The French in Dahomey were divided up at first into three groups: two formed the front and rear faces, while the remaining one formed the flank faces.

Later on four groups were organised, one for each face. The troops marched in parallel columns, and only formed square when attacked; but as the bush was thick, it was difficult for the columns to keep their proper relative positions. Shouting had to be resorted to as a means of communication, and the noise entailed by this mode of advance is a serious disadvantage.

The object in all formations, whatever their name, is to have ready a formed body of troops to bar the way to the enemy, no matter whether his attack be from the front, rear, or flank.

The double echelon formation, as used by Sir C. Egerton at the battle of Jidballi, is most effective. Rigid square can be easily and quickly formed, if need be, while should other formations become necessary, the units are marching in such a compact and ready formation that orders can be rapidly carried out. This formation is, of course, impossible in thick bush.

In "Small Wars," the method of cutting three

The Cutting of Paths when Advancing. paths through bush is advocated—the centre one for the carriers and impedimenta, while the two outside ones are to be used for flanking parties. The object to be achieved by adopting this manœuvre is not clear. If in touch with the enemy, the methods of the present day would appear sounder, by which the enemy is found by the scouts, defeated by the fighting portion of the column, while the carriers are either in zareba well in rear, or are protected in the action by their flankers and guards.

Flanking paths can never be necessary; where the savage can go, there can the well trained native soldier move and follow him. A path restricts action, shows open daylight, and men on it are lit up and present a conspicuous mark, while the savage who comes to snipe or lay an ambush has, in this path, a place and theatre of operations along which to work. Should parallel bush paths be found ready made, they are certainly useful, for by them a force can march on a broader front, but no series of parallel paths should prevent a commander from throwing out his flankers into the thick bush, for it is only from the thick bush that trouble comes.

Taking of Stockades. Should the enemy hold stockades or trenches, it has been shown that the best method of taking these works and defeating him is to keep him occupied in front with gun, maxim, and rifle fire, while a body is sent to work round one or both of his flanks and so cut his line of retreat. Fire should cease when the party has got round the flanks, and the whole force should charge the enemy in front and flank. A determined opponent will hold out behind a good stockade long enough to enable the body which is working round the flank to get well into position for the charge, and he has often suffered severely in consequence.

Should the enemy fight as the Ashantis did in 1873, or the Binis in 1897, a steady advance, with alternate short charges of sections to relieve any spot particularly hard pressed, is the best mode of driving him back. This method was very effective against the Ulians in the latter phase of the Ishan Expedition, and was also used with success in one of the reconnaissances in force carried out by No. 4 column Aro Field Force. *Fighting Without Stockades.*

The instructions issued by Sir F. Roberts in 1886 in Burma for this kind of fight are worthy of note for similar situations in other countries.

"To meet ambuscades, which usually take the form of a volley, followed by flight, and which in very dense jungle it may be impossible to discover or to guard against by flankers, His Excellency the Commander-in-Chief would like the following plan to be tried :—Supposing, for instance, the fire of the enemy to be delivered from the right, a portion of the force should be ready to dash along the road for 100 yards or so, or until some opening in the jungle offers itself. The party should then turn to the right and sweep round with a view to intercepting the enemy in his flight. A party in rear should similarly enter the jungle to their right with the same object. The centre of the column would protect the baggage or any wounded men. The different parties must be previously told off, put under the command of selected leaders, and must act with promptitude and dash. Each party must be kept in compact order, and individual fire must be prohibited except when there is a clear prospect." *Sir F. Roberts' Instructions.*

The danger of forming a camp, building a stockade, or even of halting for a few moments in any open space, say, at forked roads, in order to con- *Sentries Thrown Out into the Bush.*

sult as to the line of advance, without at once throwing out scouts or sentries into the bush, has been emphasised time after time.

Sentries concealed in the bush are no mark for the savage, who in creeping up to get a pot shot at the men in the open can easily be shot down. Even should the enemy approach in large numbers, it is much preferable and safer to resist the attack by advancing into the bush and reinforcing the sentries than by remaining in the open, and thus offering a conspicuous mark, while the exact positions of the attackers are uncertain. There is no more demoralising or hopeless feeling than the one which seizes a force condemned to volley at the enemy's smoke while occupying a position exposed to his view and fire.

The Sapoba detachment in the Benin Expedition is a case in point. Had the sailors and marines been thrown out into the bush to form a screen while the carriers cleared a space, even 400 yards square, in the centre of which shelters and a stockade (if desired) could have been erected, Commander Pritchard and the other white men might not have been killed.

There can be no doubt that the neglect of the officer commanding the escort to the late Prince Imperial, in the Zulu War of 1879, to put sentries into the long grass round his halting place, led to the surprise of the party and death of the Prince. Had any warning been given of the approach of the Zulus, the whole party could have easily withdrawn in time without hurry and confusion. Instances, unfortunately, in all wars are only too frequent in which the neglect of the most simple and obvious precautions has led to disasters and "regrettable incidents" overtaking not only small parties, but large numbers of troops. The unfortunate habit we possess of despising our enemy, of imagining "Oh, it's all right," or of relying on our luck to get well out of a hole, should we chance to fall into one, makes us casual and undoubtedly careless.

Consistent with sound dispositions, and with the fact that in order to make an enemy submit his forces must be encountered and well beaten, a commander should never do what the enemy expects. The great object of every native is to draw the white man and his troops along certain roads, and on these avenues of approach he devises and constructs elaborate obstacles and defences. Should, however, another line be chosen for the advance, and an entrance into his strongholds be effected by a path which he has neglected to defend, his confidence in himself is at once shaken. He has been morally beaten, and, although he may stand up and fight, it is at a comparative disadvantage, and in all probability with diminished forces. A great many natives will not fight at all unless they can choose their own positions. *Native Customs of War and Etiquette.*

In certain localities and amongst certain races the most scrupulous etiquette and recognised customs and laws govern the inter-tribal conflicts. With some, all operations between sunset and sunrise are forbidden, night attacks are unknown; with other tribes, districts and areas are set apart, within which limits war may be waged, while certain large farms adjoining one another, and various roads to central markets, are outside the theatre of operations. When the white man makes war, the tribes in certain cases endeavour to restrict his action and limit his times, but when he refuses to be bound by their conventions, they often complain of his unsportsmanlike conduct.

A careful reconnaissance of the various approaches into the enemy's country should therefore be made, and his idiosyncrasies and customs be studied. In the Ibeku-Olokoro Expedition the direct road into the Olokoro country was well defended. About two miles across the frontier rose a steep hill, having precipitous sides covered with impassable bush and a network of thorns. The road ran up the face of this hill, and at the crest a strong loopholed stockade had been erected across the road, its flanks rested on the edge of the precipices, and it was almost impossible to turn it. Guns were useless against it owing to the steepness of the hill, and to its being screened by bush. Pits, about three feet across and five feet deep, with a sharp stake in them and carefully concealed, were dug in the bush in front of it, and the ground for two hundred yards down the hill was a mass of needle-pointed spikes, any one of which would have penetrated even a light boot. This was a formidable obstacle, and could not have been taken without considerable loss. All the various roads into the country were found defended more or less. The approach selected was the least strongly held of all. This necessitated a detour round of about fifteen miles, and by this road the Ibeku country was entered first, in preference to that of the other tribe. The latter were much grieved that their elaborate defences had been built, as they considered, for nothing.

During Sir James Willcocks' final advance on Kumassi occurs one of the most notable instances recorded in West African warfare of outwitting the enemy.

The relief column concentrated at Bekwai. From here, the advance could be made, either direct north up the main road via Esumeja, or by

TACTICS

the more westerly road via Pekki. From Esumeja again two routes led to Kumassi, one direct along the main road, and one to the east through Kokofu. Colonel Willcocks released some prisoners and sent them to the Ashantis with a defiant message to say that the time had come when he would take and destroy their elaborate stockades on the main and Kokofu roads.

He did not let out, even to his officers, his intention of using the Pekki road, which was known to be so overgrown and difficult that the Ashantis had neglected to defend it, as compared with the other avenues of approach.

The ruse with the prisoners succeeded, and the Ashanti armies gathered on the roads through Esumeja and Kokofu, which were strongly defended by elaborate series of flanking stockades.

Not until the column had arrived within about one mile of Kumassi, where the Pekki road debouches on to the main road, was strong opposition encountered.

The methods and formations adopted in North America 150 years ago, when most of the fighting was carried out in the great forests which covered that part of the world, are very instructive. *Bush Tactics of 150 Years Ago.*

In 1755 the English and French * were engaged in the final contest for the control of North America. The country was densely wooded. The Indians, who were the allies of the French on the occasion I am about to describe, were naturally adepts in the arts of ambuscade and concealment.

The best fighters, however, in the country seemed to have been those white half breed settlers, who combined the courage and steadfast determination of the white man with the agility and cunning of the red skin.

*Wolfe and Montcalm, by Parkman.

The formation of a column on the march, and the methods used to ensure against surprises, as well as the tactics employed, will, I think, be interesting.

The battle of the Monongahela River was fought on June 9th, 1755, between a French force consisting of 72 regular soldiers, 146 Canadians and 637 Indians, officered by 36 French officers and cadets, or about 900 men under Captain Beaujeu, against an English force, commanded by General Braddock, of 86 officers, and 1,373 non-commissioned officers and men composed of regulars and provincials.

The French failed to hold the crossings of the river, owing to various causes, until it was too late, but they were on the march down to the river to lay an ambush when they encountered the English column, which had safely crossed by the ford, agreeably surprised at their good luck in getting over so easily.

The French marched with the Indians in advance (see Sketch A), and their tactics seemed to have been essentially offensive. From what one can gather they had no scouts or flankers out, and might have been ambushed had the English laid the trap. Even so, they would not, it appears, have committed the great mistake the English did, and remained on the path or road.

The theatre of the conflict, and the dispositions on the march of the English are fully described, and were as follows :—" The road from the ford ran inland for a little, then curved to the left, and followed a course parallel to the river along the base of a line of steep hills that here bordered the valley. These and all the country were buried in dense and heavy forest, choked with bushes and the trunks of fallen trees. Braddock has been charged with marching blindly into an ambuscade; but it was not so. There was no ambuscade, and had there been one, he would have found it."

It is true that he did not reconnoitre the woods very far in advance of the head of the column. Yet, with this exception, he made elaborate dispositions to prevent surprise. Several guides with six Virginian Light Horse led the way; then, a musket shot behind, came the vanguard; then three hundred soldiers under Lieut.-Col. Gage; then a large body of axemen, under Sir John Sinclair, to open the road; then two cannon with tumbrils and tool wagons, and lastly the rear guard closing the line, while flanking parties ranged the woods on both sides. This was the advance column. The main body followed on with little or no interval. The artillery and wagons moved along the road, and the troops filed through the woods close on either hand.

Numerous flanking parties were thrown out a hundred yards and more to right and left; while in the space between them and the marching column, the pack horses and cattle with their drivers made their way painfully among the trees and thickets; since, had they been allowed to follow the road, the line of march would have been too long for mutual support. A body of regulars and provincials brought up the rear.

Gage, with his advanced column, had just passed a wide and bushy ravine that crossed their path, and the van of the main column was on the point of entering it, when the guides and light horse men in the front suddenly fell back, and the engineer, Gordon, then engaged in marking out the road, saw a man dressed like an Indian, but wearing the gorget of an officer, bounding forward along the

E

EXPLANATION.

A   French and Indians when first discovered by guides.
B   Guides and six light horse.
C   Vanguard of the advanced party.
D   Advanced party commanded by Lieut.-Col. Gage.
E   Working party commanded by Sir John St. Clair, D.Q.M.G.
F   Two field pieces.
G   Waggons with powder and tools.
H   Rear guard of the advanced party.
I   Light horse leading the convoy.
K   Sailors and pioneers with a tumbril of tools, etc.
L   Three field pieces.
M   General's guard.
N   Main body upon the flanks of the convoy, with the cattle and pack horses between them and the flank guards.
O   Field piece in the rear of the convoy.
P   Rear guards.
Q   Flank guards.
R   A hollow way.
S   A hill which the Indians did most of the execution from.
T   Frazer's house.

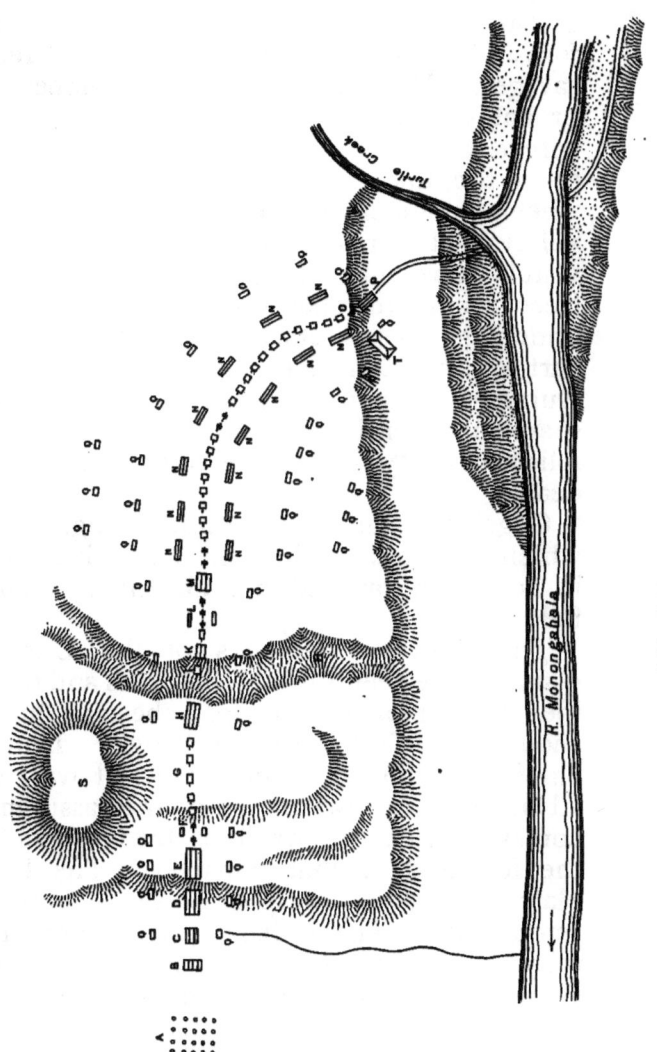

path. He stopped when he discovered the head of the column, turned, and waved his hat. The forest behind was swarming with French and savages. At the signal from the officer, who was probably Beaujeu, they yelled the war whoop, spread themselves to right and left, and opened a sharp fire, under cover of the trees. Gage's column wheeled deliberately into line, and fired several volleys with great steadiness against the now invisible assailants. Few of them were hurt, the trees caught the shot, but the noise was deafening under the dense arches of the forest. The greater part of the Canadians, to borrow the words of Dumas (Beaujeu's second in command), fled shamefully, crying, "Sauve qui peut!" Volley followed volley, and at the third Beaujeu dropped dead.

Gage's two cannon were now brought to bear, on which the Indians, like the Canadians, gave way in confusion, but did not, like them, abandon the field.

The close scarlet ranks of the English were plainly to be seen through the trees and the smoke ; they were moving forward, cheering lustily, and shouting, "God save the King." Dumas, now chief in command, thought that all was lost. "I advanced," he says, "with the assurance that comes from despair, exciting by voice and gesture the few soldiers that remained. The fire of my platoon was so sharp that the enemy seemed astonished." The Indians, encouraged, began to rally. The French officers who commanded them showed admirable courage and address ; and while Dumas and Ligneris, with the regulars, and what was left of the Canadians, held the ground in front, the savage warriors, screeching their war cries, swarmed through the forest along both flanks of the

TACTICS

English, hid behind trees, bushes, and fallen trunks, or crouched in gullies and ravines, and opened a deadly fire on the helpless soldiery, who, themselves completely visible, could see no enemy, and wasted volley after volley on the impassive trees. The most destructive fire came from a hill on the English right, where the Indians lay in multitudes, firing from their lurking places on the living target below. But the invisible death was everywhere, in front, flank, and rear. The British cheer was heard no more. The troops broke their ranks, and huddled together in a bewildered mass, shrinking from the bullets which cut them down by scores. When Braddock heard the firing in the front, he pushed forward with the main body to the support of Gage, leaving 400 men in the rear, under Sir Peter Halket, to guard the baggage. At the moment of his arrival Gage's soldiers had abandoned their two cannon, and were falling back to escape the concentrated fire of the Indians. Meeting the advancing troops, they tried to find cover behind them. This threw the whole into confusion. The men of the two regiments became mixed together, and in a short time the entire force, except the Virginians and the troops left with Halket, were massed in several dense bodies within a small space of ground, facing some one way, some another, and all alike exposed without shelter to the bullets that pelted them like hail. Both men and officers were new to this blind and frightful warfare of the savage in his native woods. . . . The Virginians alone were equal to the emergency. Fighting behind trees like the Indians themselves, they might have held the enemy in check till order could be restored, had not Braddock, furious at a proceeding that shocked all his ideas of courage and discipline, ordered them with oaths to form into line.

A body of them, under Captain Waggoner, made a dash for a fallen tree lying in the woods far out toward the lurking places of the Indians, and, crouching behind the huge trunk, opened fire; but the regulars, seeing smoke among the bushes, mistook their best friends for the enemy, shot at them from behind, killed many, and forced the rest to return. A few of the regulars also tried in their clumsy way to fight behind trees; but Braddock beat them with his sword, and compelled them to stand with the rest, an open mark for the Indians. The panic increased. The soldiers crowded together, and the "bullets spent themselves in a mass of human bodies." So it got worse and worse, the artillery doing great damage to the trees, and little to the enemy, the soldiers loading and firing mechanically into the air at times, and often into their comrades, many of whom were killed. The ground became encumbered with the dead and wounded. The roar of the cannon and muskets, added to the yells from the throats of the 600 unseen savages, combined to form a "chaos of anguish and terror scarcely paralleled even in Indian warfare." Braddock was everywhere, storming and cheering like one demented. He had four horses shot under him, and mounted a fifth. The account of the splendid gallantry of the various officers and their terrible slaughter is pitiable reading. Out of 86, 63 were killed or disabled. Braddock then commanded a retreat; the soldiers broke and fled helter skelter, leaving everything—wounded comrades, baggage, cannon—all to the Indians. It was now that Braddock himself was shot down, but was carried off by a few devoted followers. The Indians stayed to scalp and loot, and the French had had enough, so the English were not followed. All dead and wounded were scalped. About a dozen

TACTICS

prisoners were taken, and these the Indians stripped naked, and burnt to death that evening on return to their camp.

The English, as before stated, lost 63 officers out of 86, while out of 1,373 men only 459 came off unharmed, showing a casualty list of 73 per cent. amongst the officers, and 66 per cent. amongst the Non-Coms. and men. The French casualty returns show how little they suffered.

Three officers were killed and four wounded. Of the regular soldiers only four were wounded. The Canadians suffered five casualties. The loss of the Indians, who won the victory, was twenty-seven, a total percentage of under five for the entire force.

This is a very instructive fight. The arrangement of the column to guard against surprise and ambush, on the march, could not have been better, but as it had to fight a battle, it might, perhaps, have been differently arranged. All the troops which could have been spared should have marched at the head to form the fighting force, while the duty of the remainder should have been to protect the wagons and pack horses. As will be seen from Sketch A, the wagons marched on the road, guarded on each side by detachments of the main body, as it was called, and these amounted to a considerable body of men; outside these again were the cattle and pack horses, also protected by flank guards. There appears to be a waste of strength by having two bodies of troops, one inside the other, guarding the convoy. Of what use were the "Main Body" troops? Augment the flank troops if necessary, and send all the remaining men to the front.

Either it was not deemed wise in those days to park the convoy, leave it with a sufficient guard, and proceed against the enemy with a purely fighting force, or else the disposition was not thought of. When the ford was found undefended by the French, had General Braddock parked his convoy on the south bank of the river at the ford, left, say, 400 men to defend it, as was subsequently done during the action, and had he advanced against the French (by whom he knew he was going to be opposed that day) with a purely fighting column of some 900 men, his chances of success would perhaps have been enhanced. It does not appear from the account that the convoy was seriously attacked during the fight, but there can be no doubt that its protection caused General Braddock anxiety, as it was bound to do, and had he been free from this, and been able, with a purely fighting column, to turn all his attention to the enemy, a defeat such as took place might not have been chronicled. The English overthrow was due undoubtedly to the action of the Indians. The French soldiers and Canadians were content to remain on or near the path and ply the English with fire. The English adopted the same tactics, and owing at first to their superior fire they nearly caused the rout of the French, but once the Indians spread into the bush and began " bush tactics " proper, the English defeat was a certainty. The Virginians, who of all the force alone appeared to understand the situation, were not allowed to adopt the only methods which they knew should be resorted to, and so the wretched soldiery huddled together in the open and presented a conspicuous target, into which their ever-moving unseen enemy could empty their guns with impunity.

The French casualties show how hopeless the English tactics were, and how useless it is to bombard the bush.

TACTICS 55

In direct contrast, in the way of tactics, to the foregoing was the Guasimas fight in the Cuban War in 1898.*

Guasimas Fight, Cuban War.

The Rough Riders, numbering 534 men, under command of Colonel Wood, with whom was Lieut.-Colonel Roosevelt, were ordered to advance from Siboney, where General Wheeler's army had landed, along a trail bordered by thick bushes and grass, and to join another column on their right at Guasimas. The two columns advanced along trails which, starting some distance apart, joined at the apex of the letter V inverted. The apex was Guasimas. There was a valley between the trails, and the bushes were so thick on both sides that it was not possible at any time for the columns to communicate until they arrived at Guasimas, some three miles from the starting points of each column.

The enemy was reported entrenched at Guasimas. The Rough Riders were without horses, some half-dozen officers only being mounted. The order of march was as follows :—Captain Capron, with his troop of 60 men, acted as advanced guard. First marched two Cuban scouts. One hundred yards in rear of them came the " point," consisting of five picked men and two sergeants. Following the point at a distance of 150 yards came the troop in single file. No flankers were thrown out, owing to the dense undergrowth and the tangle of vines, that, stretching from tree to tree, and interlacing with the bushes below, made it a physical impossibility for anyone to move off the beaten trail.

The column followed the advanced guard, strung out in single file, headed by Colonel Wood, Lieut.-Colonel Roosevelt, and three other staff officers.

With some brief halts they moved forward for

*Cuban and Porto-Rican Campaign, by Richard Harding Davis, F.R.G.S.

about an hour and a half, when a report came in to the commanding officer that the scouts had seen the outposts of the enemy. A halt was ordered, and Colonel Wood rode forward to reconnoitre. The place where the head of the column halted was marked by the narrowing of the trail, which dropped sharply to the front. On the left side was a stout barbed wire fence of five strands, shutting off fields of high grass, blocked every fifty yards or so by great barricades of tangled trees and chaparral. On the right the bush was so impenetrable, and impossible for any sustained or organised advance, that troops, which were at first ordered to that flank, had to be withdrawn. Wood discovered the enemy, and ordered Capron to take his troop down the trail itself. G troop was ordered into the bush on the right of the trail, two were sent down into the hollow on the right to prolong the line, and join up, if possible, with the other column, and two more troops moved into the bush to the left, and formed line.

A sharp fire was now opened on the Rough Riders by the enemy, who seemed to be not more than 60 or 70 yards away, and their fire being low at once caused casualties, although nothing was seen of them. G troop struggled forward through the dense maze for a short distance until they came to a small open space, on the far side of which was an impenetrable wall of vines and undergrowth, concealing their assailants. The troop here halted and returned the fire which came from the far side of the opening. The troop could not now advance. On the right they could hear heavy firing, showing that the other column had become engaged.

Lieut.-Col. Roosevelt now came up, and seeing that an advance was impossible, ordered the troop across the trail to the left, where it reinforced the

TACTICS

other two troops. He then took command and directed the extreme left of the line formed by these three and Capron's troop. The four of them under Col. Wood endeavoured then to envelop the enemy's right. In the meantime the two troops on the right had managed to get down into the valley and join up with the other column.

The advances were now made in rushes, volley firing was used, and the fire directed low and at the places from which the enemy's fire appeared to come. The fire discipline was excellent. It was terribly trying work and sapped the men's strength. The grass was as hot as a steam bath, and the thorns and sward-like grass tore their clothes and lacerated their skin.

The methods adopted by the various men during the short and sharp rushes showed their previous training and bringing up. The Eastern man broke from cover and rushed crouching to the next bit of shelter ahead to which he was directed, like a man "trying to get out of the rain"; the Western hunters and trappers wriggled and dodged from one bit of cover to another, from bush to bush, from tree-trunk to tree-trunk, came up and fell into line with the rest, never having exposed themselves once during the advance.

Wonderful line was kept, owing to the individual intelligence, keenness, and readiness of spirit being of a high order amongst both men and officers.

This advance through dense bush ended in a final charge across open fields, and the Spaniards took to flight.

The Spaniards state they had 4,000 men engaged, while the Rough Riders, as already stated, numbered 534, of whom eight were killed and 34 wounded.

This is a very interesting bush fight, and more approximates as regards the armament of both sides engaged to what we might expect a bush fight in the present day would be between two well-armed foes, than do the engagements which we are accustomed to, where we have been well armed and our opponents badly, in comparison. The Spaniards used smokeless powder, which rendered their concealment all the more effectual, and had the Rough Riders been content to adopt any but the most vigorous and offensive tactics, they could never have hoped to succeed.

Disadvantages of Defensive Position. It rather points to the uselessness of taking up a defensive position in the bush, unless a great deal of time can be spared to so clear the forest in front as to give a sufficient field of fire. Time must also be allowed for the preparation of obstacles and entanglements which will not obstruct the view or mask the fire. Even then the enemy will work round the flanks, and it will be extremely difficult to plan trenches and prepare the bush so as to protect the flanks and defeat turning movements. The attackers have everything in their favour: all their movements are concealed, they can concentrate at any point in strength under cover, they can make a great show against part or all of the defensive position with a few troops comparatively, while utterly unknown to the defence a large force may be despatched to attack the flank. Again, the defence is more or less restricted to the quiescent rôle, counter-attacks will be difficult to carry out, and should they be undertaken may waste their energy and strength on a useless object, and find that, before they can be withdrawn and the men collected, the presence of the troops would have been more usefully employed elsewhere. In fact it might be quite possible for an attack to draw the defence on to a counter-attack against a carefully prepared ambush, so that the presence of these troops may be withdrawn from the decisive point of attack.

Bush warfare, therefore, between two well-armed and well-disciplined forces will open up a larger field for surprises, feints, ambuscades, bluff and "slimness," than, if possible, ordinary fighting in any European country.

CHAPTER II.

SIZE AND COMPOSITION OF COLUMNS.

Size of Columns.
IT is generally conceded that several comparatively small columns, operating either separate lines of advance, or following one another along the same road with an interval of 24 hours between them, is a much more simple and effective way of moving against a bush enemy than by employing one huge cumbersome column. It must be remembered that each man in single file takes up about two yards of path at least, and that a large force with its attendant carriers will be so strung out when once on the march that it is quite possible the rear guard may not arrive in camp until some 8 or 10 hours after the advanced guard. During the march of the column which finally relieved Kumassi in 1900, the force of 1,000 soldiers and 1,700 carriers was so lengthy, owing to bad roads and incessant rains, that the rear guard one night did not get into camp until nearly 2 a.m. The size of this column was, however, dictated by necessity, and was only for a short duration, some three or four days, and never could have been maintained for any length of time.

A column should be just large enough to defeat any force it encounters, and be capable of a vigorous pursuit; add a few more as a margin for safety and eventualities, and then keep this body intact. There might be danger perhaps in splitting it up. Other columns of the same size might be

SIZE, &c., OF COLUMNS

employed on other lines of approach or in other districts, and so divide the enemy's forces and prevent him from having a safe and quiet section of his country to which, after defeat, the chiefs could repair and re-organize the resistance.

The Achin war of 1874 furnishes an example of the danger of splitting up a column.* Splitting up Columns

Two separate columns were sent out from Kota-Raja to make a combined movement to capture the village of Longbatta : one was to move directly on the town, while the other, making a detour, was to attack the right of the place.

The direct attack in the thick bush bore too much to its right, and being delayed by obstacles, brought up at Panjaret much exhausted, it never advanced beyond this point. The other column reached Longbatta and took it after some fighting. It then moved against Lung. The Achinese immediately began to re-occupy Longbatta, and now the dangerous division of force was made, for a portion of the column was sent back to occupy Longbatta and deny it to the enemy, while the remainder went on and captured Lung. Here they were attacked by a superior force of the enemy and suffered severely in retreat to Longbatta, being nearly annihilated.

The enemy's *moral* is at once raised by a retreat of this nature. One disastrous retreat, even of a small force, counteracts the effects of several previous victories.

A force of 200 men might be ample in certain situations, whereas in others it might easily find itself in grave jeopardy. In most cases, however, a column of from 300 to 500 men will be found strong enough with which to meet any bush enemy.

* "Small Wars," by Major C. E. Callwell.

EXPLANATION.

A   The French and Indians skulking behind trees round the British.
F   The two field pieces of the advance party abandoned.
C, D, E, H, K, M, N, Q   The whole body of the British joined with little or no order, but endeavouring to make fronts towards the enemy's fire.
L   The three field pieces of the main body.
P   The rear guard divided (round the rear of the convoy now closed up) behind trees, having been attacked by a few Indians.

N.B.—The dispositions on both sides continued for about two hours nearly as here represented, the British endeavouring to cover the guns (F) and to gain the hill (S) to no purpose. The British were at length beat from the guns (L). The General was wounded soon after. They were at last beat across the hollow way (R), and made no further stand. The retreat was full of confusion and hurry, but after a few miles there was a body got ready to rally.

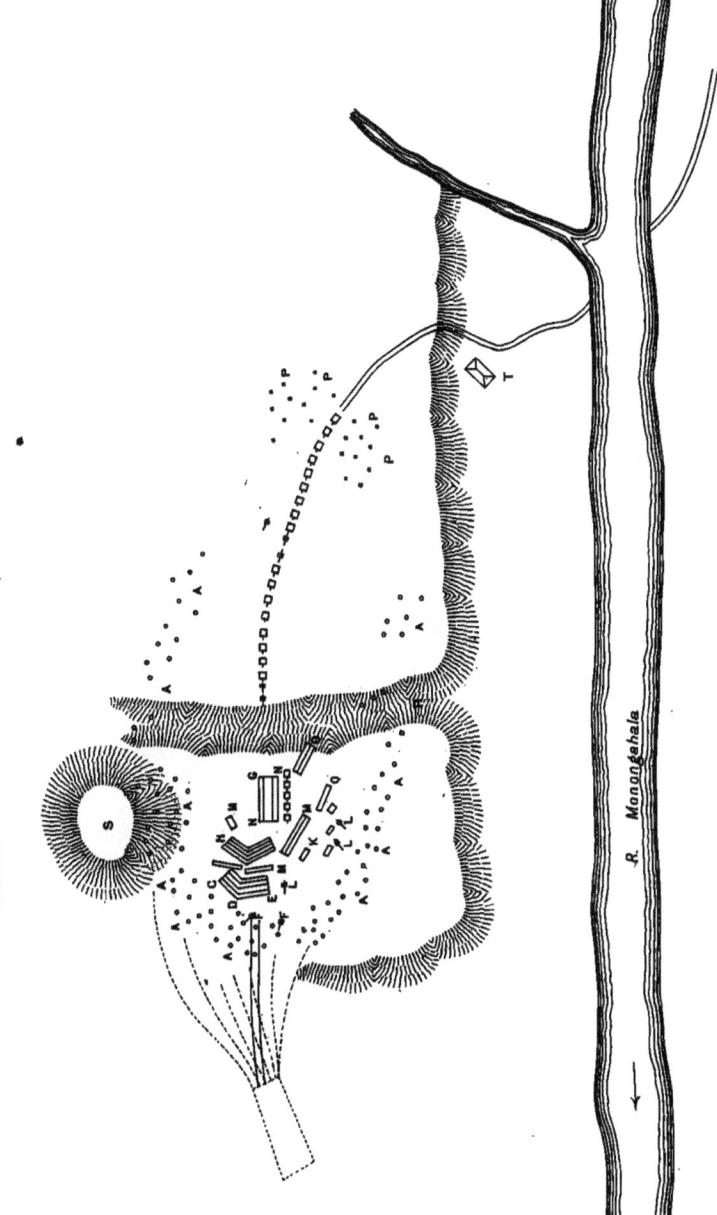

ACHIN WAR, 1874.
CAPTURE OF LONGBATTA.

No 7

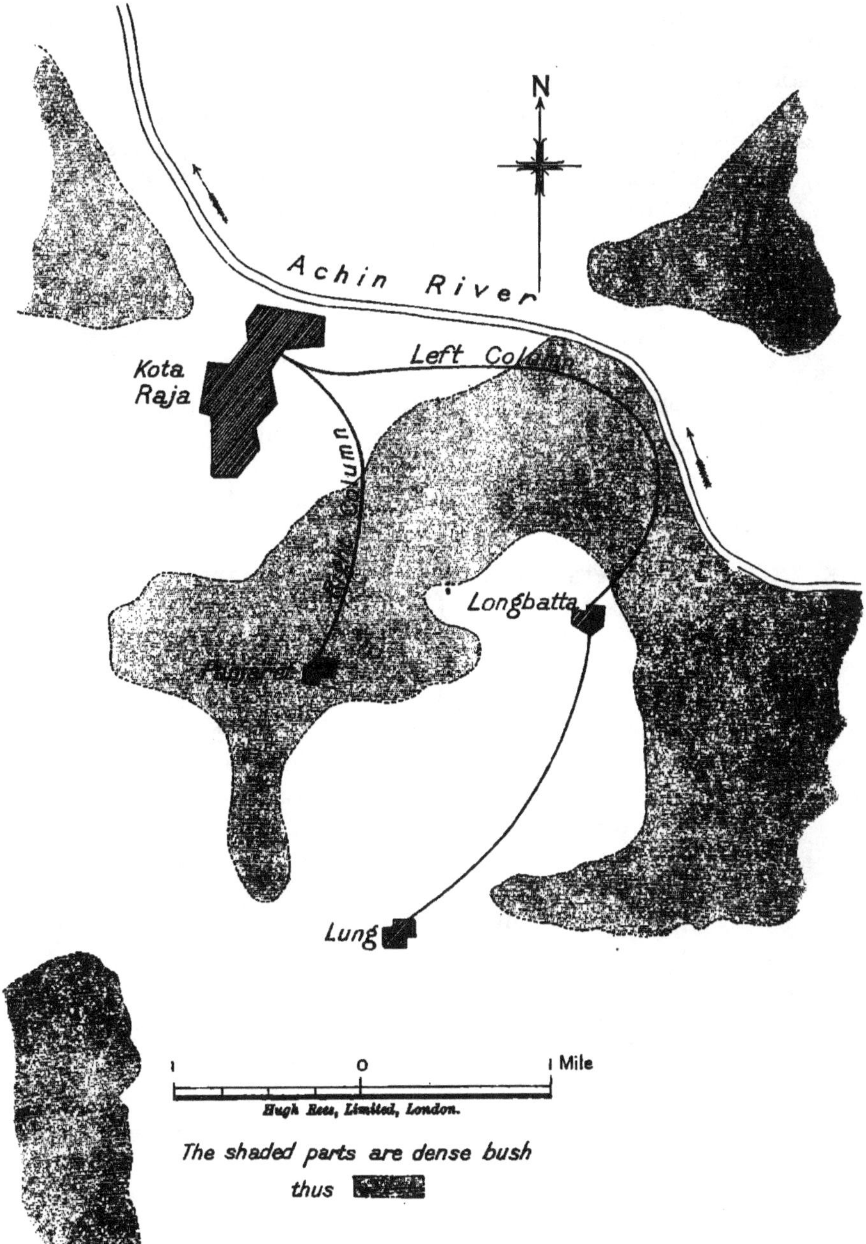

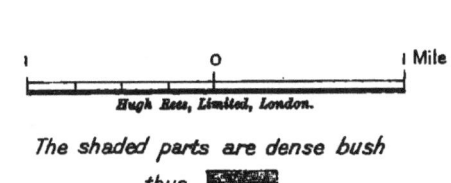

BUSH WARFARE

The Largest Column which can be Employed Usefully.

The largest purely fighting force which can be usefully employed in one column in bush was one commanded by Lieut.-Col. Morland at the taking of Kokofu. It consisted of three 2·95-in. guns, two 7-pounders, 800 infantry or seven companies and their maxims; even this column will take up, with the carriers necessary for a week's work, from two to three miles of bush path.

The disposition of this column on the march was as follows:—

ADVANCED GUARD.*

Major Melliss commanding.
½ Company West African Regiment under Captain St. Hill acting as scouts.
E Company 1st W.A.F.F.
F Company 1st W.A.F.F.

MAIN BODY.

50 pioneers under Captain Neal, Transport Officer.
The guns and escort (½ Company W.A. Regiment).
Commanding Officer and Staff.
Personal escort of D. Company 1st W.A.F.F.
Dressing station with 2 medical officers and 12 hammocks and stretchers, Dr. Buée in charge.
½ Company 3rd W.A.F.F. under Lieut. Shortland.
1 Company W.A. Rifles under Capt. Tighe, D.S.O.
½ E Company 2nd W.A.F.F., under Capt. Greer.
Reserve Ammunition Column.
Field Hospital of 18 hammocks and stretchers, with 2 medical officers, Dr. Langstaff in charge.

REAR GUARD.

Major Beddoes Commanding.
½ E Company 2nd W.A.F.F. under Captain Monck-Mason.
B Company 2nd W.A.F.F.

*"The Ashanti Campaign of 1900," by Captain C. H. Armitage, D.S.O., and Lieut.-Col. A. F. Montanaro.

SIZE, &c., OF COLUMNS

It has often been the case that the advanced guard of a large column has fought a successful action and the rear guard has been unaware of the fact.

In Burma, columns were seldom more than 300 men with one or two guns, and these were large enough for safety's sake, for no disaster during the three years' fighting overtook a column.

The strongest column which has been employed under one command was that which, at the close of the 1900 Ashanti campaign operated in the country north-west of Kumassi, and fought the battle of Obassa, on 30th September, 1900, which practically finished the campaign. This column was commanded by Sir James Willcocks in person, and consisted of three 75-millimetre guns, two 7-pounder guns, and 1,200 infantry, with their complement of maxims. A column of this size would seldom be employed unless it was intended to send detachments out from it as it proceeded, to scour the country on either side of the general line of advance. This was done when Captain Carleton with two companies was detached from what was called the Berekum column, to effect the capture of the Ashanti Chief, Kobina Cherri, who was reported to be in hiding in a village off the main line of advance. This detachment joined the parent column after an absence of some ten or twelve hours. As a rule the ordinary column for bush work is something under 500 fighting men strong.

The disposition of the troops on the march for Sir J. Willcocks' large column was as follows :—

Two 75-millimetre guns and four companies infantry under Lieut.-Col. Montanaro formed the advanced guard. Major Mellis, with one of these guns and three companies of infantry, formed a support to Col. Montanaro. Major Cobbe, with 350 men, had the reserve ammunition and rations under his charge, and these composed the main body. A rear guard of two 7-pounder guns and 200 infantry, under Captain Greer, completed the column. The commanding officer Sir James Willcocks, marched near the head of the support, and he retained under his direct orders the Sikh contingent, some 70 men, to be used as he thought necessary in case of emergency. As transpired, this body of men, thrown into the Obassa fight at exactly the right moment, converted, by their staunchness and dash, a hesitating charge into a headlong rush, which the enemy were powerless to stem.

Columns Aro Field Force. In the Aro Campaign, 1901-2, under the direction of Col. A. F. Montanaro, the country was entered by four columns to start with, the idea, of course, being to split up the Aro forces. This nation was composed of fourteen families, and dominated a country 120 miles by 90 miles in area. The force employed numbered 1,745 officers and men with 2,100 carriers, and was divided up as follows :— (See Map on page 160.)

Column No. 1.—One 75-millimetre gun, one maxim, 16 Europeans, and 300 native rank and file under Captain A. T. Jackson, Worcester Regiment, concentrated at Oguta and marched to Oweri.

Column No. 2.—Two 75-millimetre guns, two maxims, 19 Europeans, and 451 native rank and file under Major A. M. N. Mackenzie, R.A., concentrated at Ungwana and marched into the Ahoffia country.

Column No. 3.—One 75-millimetre gun, two maxims, 20 Europeans, and 375 native rank and file under Lieutenant-Colonel A. Festing, C.M.G., D.S.O., Royal Irish Rifles, concentrated at Akwete

SIZE, &c., OF COLUMNS

and marched to Oweri, was joined by No. 1 column, and marched to Bendi, joining hands with No. 2.

No. 4.—One 75-millimetre gun, one 7-pounder, one rocket tube and two maxims, 19 Europeans, one native officer, and 479 rank and file under Major Heneker, concentrated at Itu and feinted towards Aro-Chuku.

This column was subsequently reinforced by the addition of the majority of No. 2 column, and Aro-Chuku, the capital, taken. Colonel Festing's column later on marched into the capital from the north.

Had one huge and unwieldy column penetrated the Aro country it would probably have taken a much longer time to conquer than it did under Colonel Montanaro's dispositions. The enemy would have fought and fallen back before the troops, chiefs and the instigators of various massacres would have been exceedingly hard to catch, and altogether the Aro nation would not have been so soon brought to their knees by a manifestation of overwhelming strength as was the case by using converging columns. The enemy strenuously opposed the troops and suffered severe punishment, without which, of course, they would not have so soon recognized that resistance was hopeless. Chiefs wanted for crime, ran from one district to another, and in none was safety and repose where they could, after suffering defeat, re-organize their forces.

After the concentration at Aro-Chuku, other columns of like numbers and composition were made up and sent out to pacify the country, but the main scope of the expedition was in the defeating of the Aro forces guarding their capital and " Long Juju." The dispositions of Colonel Montanaro were certainly sound, and the size of the columns judicious and handy.

BUSH WARFARE

Benin, 1895.

In the Benin Expedition in 1897, to punish the king and people for the massacre of Mr. Phillips and his party, Admiral Rawson was able to employ marines, sailors, and native troops to effect his purpose. His objective was Benin City, the principal town of the country. It was some twenty-four miles from the river at Warrigi, where his ships and force could rendezvous.

He decided to march against the city with a fighting force capable of defeating the enemy, and holding the place when captured. Two smaller forces were sent, one to each flank, to feint, and prevent the Binis from concentrating all their strength against his real advance.

His dispositions and the size of each of the separate bodies operating were quite different from any other expedition.

To Gwatto and Gilli Gilli (see map) he detached the *Philomel, Barrosa,* and *Widgeon,* with six canoes manned by friendly natives. This force was under Captain O'Callaghan, R.N. He landed a force of 80 bluejackets and marines, took and destroyed Gwatto, was attacked by large numbers of the enemy, but held his ground, and created the diversion necessary.

At the same time Captain M'Gill was sent in command of the *Phœbe, Alecto,* and *Magpie* up the Jamieson river to the east, and landing at Sapoba with 65 bluejackets and marines, marched a short distance inland. The Binis opposed this small force vigorously, and it suffered severely, but undoubtedly held large numbers of the Bini warriors down in that part of the country, and prevented them from joining in the defence of their city. The main column did not start until the Gwatto and Sapoba contingents had come in touch with the enemy, and then, having landed at

SIZE, &c., OF COLUMNS 67

Warrigi, it pushed along the Ologbo, Ogegi road, to Benin city.

It consisted of sailors, marines, and native soldiers belonging to the Protectorate Force. The two former were divided up as follows :—

- 1st Division—150 sailors and 66 marines, and 4 maxims.
- 2nd Division—150 sailors and 78 marines, and 4 maxims.
- A Carrier Column of 98 sailors, 66 marines, and 4 maxims, and finally a Marine Company, consisting of 100 men with 2 maxims. The total amounting to 708 white men.

The Protectorate Troops with this main column consisted of 4 companies of native soldiers, 2 7-pounders, 2 maxims, and 1 rocket tube, while an irregular corps of 50 scouts was raised specially for the expedition. The above force was divided up into three columns, called the Advance Column, 1st Division and 2nd Division. As the distance from the water to Benin City was only some twenty miles, the difficulties regarding lines of communication were not great. The Advanced Column was to bear the brunt of the fighting, supported by the 1st Division, while the 2nd Division formed an advanced depot nine miles from Ologbo, the advanced base, and was to guard the line of communications. The Advanced Column was composed and marched as follows :—

Scouts
½ Co. N.C.P., Force under Capt. Carter
Maxim
Rocket Tube
2½ Cos. Niger Coast Protectorate Force
Maxim

BENIN EXPE

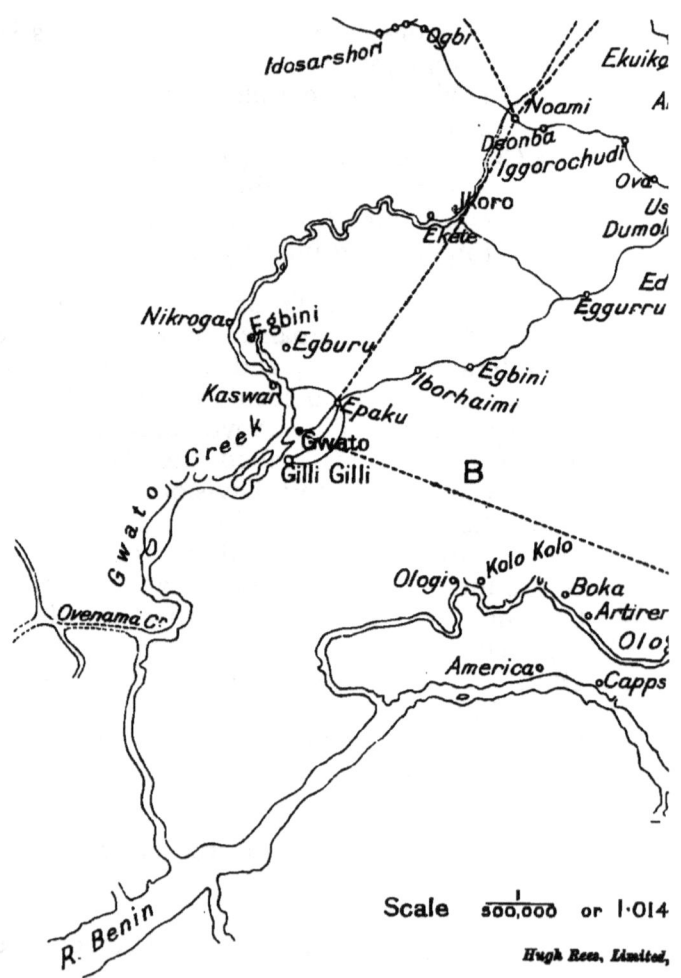

DITION, 1897.

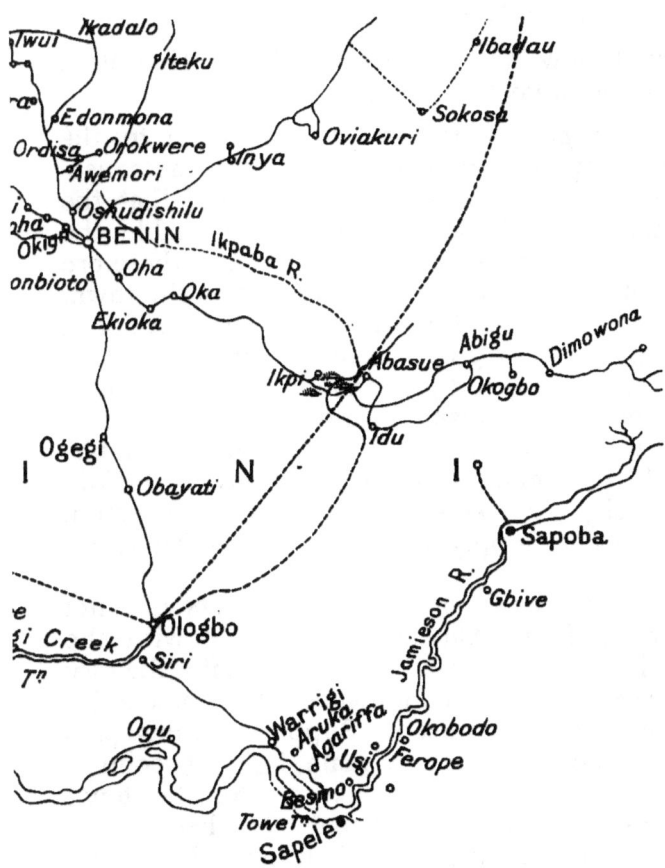

Inches to 8 Miles

London.

2 7-pounder guns
1 Co. Marines
Baggage Guard 12 Marines
Maxim
4 Scouts
1 Co. N.C.P. Force.

Colonel (now Major-General Sir Bruce Hamilton, K.C.B.) was in command.

All water had to be carried, and owing to the amount of opposition encountered, and the consequent slow rate of advance, it was found that the water carried would not be sufficient to enable the force to reach Benin City. A depôt was therefore formed at Ogegi, some twelve miles from the town, all impedimenta and extra carriers left under a sufficient force to guard them, a purely fighting force was formed, and just enough water carried to enable this force to reach Benin.

The water just held out, although all ranks suffered from being put on a short ration; luckily after the city was taken, the Bini forces dispersed, and the water supply of the town was found unguarded.

The Gwatto and Sapoba detachments did not advance to Benin City and co-operate with the main column. They were withdrawn after the city was taken, having accomplished the objects for which they were organised. Supply columns proceeded in the wake of the main fighting column along the same road, and pushed on for the town as soon as word was received that it had been taken.

In this campaign the main fighting column was under 500 strong. It was supported by another body of not more than 220 men; they were all white men, however. The Sapoba and Gwatto bodies, all white men, were each well under one hundred.

SIZE, &c., OF COLUMNS

They were never intended to advance inland, but these comparatively few men held their own on the defensive against large numbers of the enemy, who had no idea that they were not the advanced portions of the main force.

ASHANTI CAMPAIGN, 1895-96.

This was a bloodless campaign, and therefore it is impossible to draw many lessons from it. One point about the advance to Kumassi is interesting, and that is the size and arrangement of the column during the last stage of the advance. It was thought that the probability of an encounter with the enemy just before entering Kumassi was far from unlikely, and therefore, with this fact in view, the following column was formed. First marched Major Baden-Powell with his corps of 860 native levies, divided up into three parties, a central one and two flanking ones on bye roads.

The distance of these levies in front of the advanced guard was variable. The column then followed as under :—

ADVANCED GUARD.*

2 Companies Gold Coast Houssas and maxim. Interval of ¼ mile.
Communication was kept up by dropping men from the Houssas.

MAIN BODY.

Special Service Corps.
2 guns.
Maxim.

*" Downfall of Prempeh," by Major Baden-Powell.

Head Quarter Staff.
½ Bearer Company.
6 Companies 2nd West Yorkshire Regiment.
2 guns.
2 rockets.
½ bearer company.
Ammunition column.
Baggage column.
Supply column.
Field hospital.

} One company 2nd West India Regiment was distributed by half sections throughout this portion of the column.

REAR GUARD.

2 companies 2nd West Yorkshire Regiment.
Lagos Hausas and maxim.

The length of the column, exclusive of levies, advanced, and rear guards, was nearly nine miles. It would have been better to split the force into two parts—a purely fighting portion and a baggage column, with sufficient troops attached to it to ensure its safety if attacked. One company appears to be a very small baggage guard. The advantage and advisability of marching levies in such large numbers in front of troops is open to question. Had the Ashanti warriors been found that day barring the road with the same pluck, and showing the fighting instincts which distinguished them in 1873 and in 1900, these levies would, in all probability, have been a source of grave embarrassment to the regular troops. I propose to deal with the question of levies in a future chapter, so shall leave this question at present.

Order of March of Large Force. In Colonel Montanaro's book on bush fighting he gives in detail the order of march for a force of 60 Europeans, 1,200 native troops, and 1,438 carriers, for a seven days' march. He divides his force into two parts, a fighting portion consisting of

SIZE, &c., OF COLUMNS

800 men, and a supply column composed of the carriers and 400 troops as escort.

The supply column, marching in rear and independently of the fighting column, should, however, use every endeavour to reach it at night and encamp with it, owing to the fact that it contains the baggage, food, and reserve of ammunition required daily by the troops. One day's rations should, however, always be carried by officers and men in case the supply column is unable to get up in time. This separating the force into two is undoubtedly an advantageous arrangement when such a large number of men are employed on one path, but for a small column it is not so necessary. Anyone who has marched with a column in single file, and who has suffered from the continual concertina-like movement which pervades it, necessitating a halt one moment and a run the next to catch up the men in front so as to prevent a gap, can readily see that the longer the column, the more pronounced is this contortion. It is exceedingly trying to anyone subjected to it, even when lightly laden, but to a carrier with his 60lbs. load it is heartbreaking and soon wears him out.

The tired carrier will cause gaps in the long column owing to his inability to keep up, and the chances are that the break is where there are no troops; should the enemy cut in at this place serious confusion and loss of carriers is the result. As a rule the enemy expends his whole strength against the fighting column, and having been defeated, the supplies, with their escort, can advance unmolested at an easy pace. Even should they be attacked, the escort ought to have no difficulty in beating the enemy off, and then the march can be resumed.

The dispositions for the march of the above force

are found in Colonel Montanaro's book, and are as follows :—

ADVANCED GUARD.
2½ Companies Infantry.
1 m/m Gun and Escort.
2 Maxims.
Stretcher Party.

- Scouts } ½ Company
- Point
- O.C. Advanced Guard } 1 Company
- Maxim
- m/m Gun
- 1 Section Infantry Escort
- Medical Officer
- Stretcher Party
- 1 Company
- Maxim

O.C. Column

MAIN BODY.
2½ Companies Infantry
1 m/m Gun and Escort
2 Maxims
Bearer Company

- 1 Company
- Maxim
- m/m Gun
- Escort, 1 Section Infantry
- Maxim
- 1½ Companies
- P.M.O.
- Bearer Company

REAR GUARD.
1 Company Infantry
1 7-Pounder and Escort
1 Maxim

- 7-Pounder Gun
- Escort 1 Section Infantry.
- Maxim
- 1 Company

Total :—3 guns, 5 maxims, 6¾ companies infantry divided into 27 sections, or about 800 men.

Now for the Supply Column, to which is told off one 7-pounder gun, two maxims, and 3¼ companies or 13 sections. If two sections be used as advanced guard with one maxim, one section escort to gun, and one section rear guard, it leaves nine sections

SIZE, &c., OF COLUMNS

to be divided up amongst the carriers. What is required in camp first should be placed at the head of the column, which might be composed as follows :—

>2 Sections
>Maxim
>½ Rice Carriers
>Baggage Carriers
>½ Reserve Ammunition
>7-pounder Gun
>1 Section Escort
>Remainder of Carriers
>Maxim
>1 Section

The nine sections should be distributed equally throughout the carriers by $\frac{1}{2}$ sections. This is a slightly different arrangement to that suggested by Colonel Montanaro; I have found, however, the above work well, and therefore give it instead of his distribution.

The above force would take up about $4\frac{1}{2}$ miles of road in single file, if used in one column.

It would be wrong to say that a force should never march in one column, but should always be divided up into a fighting portion, distinct from that of the carriers, for in a great number of instances, when small columns have been employed, the carriers have marched behind the troops detailed to do the fighting, but with no interval between the two portions. Should the whereabouts of the enemy be uncertain, and the probability of an encounter equally so, it will mean a long day's scouting, at the rate of perhaps one mile an hour, often less. This pace is very hard on carriers, and the splitting up of the column into two parts would probably be advantageous. Again, should the enemy's position and line of stockades be known, say half mile on the far side of a river, it might be a good plan to march altogether to the water, park the convoy with a guard on the near bank, and proceed against the enemy with the fighting portion of the force. Dispositions must be governed by circumstances.

THE GERMAN OPERATIONS AGAINST THE BONDELSZWARTS AND HEREROS, WHICH COMMENCED IN OCTOBER, 1903.*

German S.W. Africa. This campaign, more than the Cuban one, demonstrates the difficulties which attend combatants in bush warfare, when each are well armed, and know how to use their rifles. The Hereros were supposed to be able to put 6,000 men in the field, all armed with breech-loading rifles of the Mauser (1871) type, or of equally good arms of English manufacture. They were skilful shots, and, combining an aptitude for guerilla warfare with an accurate knowledge of their country, and plentiful supplies of ammunition, were an enemy such as we have not, up to this, encountered in the bush. The uplands of the country in the north, which was the theatre of operations, are healthy, covered with dense bush and grass, but affording good grazing for horses and beasts of burden. In the south the country is mountainous; steep walls of mountain impede free movement, and here also the vegetation is luxuriant. Swakopmund, the port on the coast, was the landing place for reinforcements and stores sent from Germany, and the troops, etc., were conveyed thence across the sixty

*United Service Magazine.

or seventy miles of sandy waste, between the sea and the hills, by rail. I do not, in quoting this campaign, intend to do more than refer to the size and composition of the columns which the Germans employed in the Onjatu and Waterberg fights, and the methods which they considered suitable to cope with the situation on each occasion. When the rising broke out, the total effective strength of the Protectorate force was 44 officers and 692 non-commissioned officers and men, and they were scattered about the country in detachments. Troops were hurried out from Germany. The first real move of the campaign was made by Major Von Glasenapp, who, with a force of 22 officers and 476 men, started from Onjatu on 1st April to attack the enemy in Onjatu Hills. He was to co-operate with Colonel Leutwein, who, with a force of 7 companies, 2 field batteries, a mountain battery, a machine-gun detachment, and 50 Witbois, or Bastards, a total force of 1,272 men, 600 horses, 400 mules, 980 draught animals, 450 animals for slaughter, 49 wagons, each drawn by 20 oxen, and carrying four weeks' provisions, marched from Okahandja on 7th April against the Onjatu Hills, and hoped to co-operate successfully with Major Von Glasenapp, although separated from him by fifty miles of dense bush. This is a very unwieldy column for bush work. In single file its length must have been very great. The troops required to guard the wagons and animals left comparatively few in advance to cope with the enemy. Von Glasenapp fell into an ambush while on the march. The enemy allowed his mounted troops to pass, and attacked the long column in the centre and rear. He managed to extricate his men and fall back on Onjatu. On 21st April he had to abandon this place, and retired to Otjihaenena, having lost since the start, from sickness and fighting, 63 per cent. of his officers, and 39 per cent. of his men.

Col. Leutwein on 9th April came in touch with the Hereros near a defile of the hills, and after a nine hours' fight defeated the enemy, who dispersed, leaving only a few cattle in the hands of the victors. He pursued what he considered the bulk of the fugitives, leaving his convoy behind under a strong guard, but unfortunately fell into an ambush on 13th April. After ten hours' fighting, the force, being short of ammunition, fell back to the convoy at Otjosasu. Thus ended the first phase. The troops suffered greatly from fever and typhus.

The principal point to note in considering this, the first phase, is the want of precaution taken during the advances. Each column was ambushed. It is a very difficult and slow business this hunting for the enemy during an advance. In thick bush, if proper precautions are taken and careful scouting carried out, it will rarely be possible for a force to advance more than three-quarters of a mile an hour; as the bush becomes more open, so will the pace become quicker, but at the best of times $1\frac{1}{2}$ miles an hour is fast work. The course pursued of operating against the enemy with two columns did not give much chance of dealing the Hereros an irreparable blow. They had numerous roads by which to vanish should the tide go against them, and, what is more, by which to get their cattle away, their only means of subsistence. It is of course an exceedingly difficult matter, and almost an impossibility, to block all roads. But had five or six columns been used, each about 300 strong, operating from Okahandja, Owiumbo, Onjatu, Konoro, Otjihaenena, and one from the south; had these places been provisioned and left with sufficient troops to guard them, and had the columns then marched

SIZE, &c., OF COLUMNS

against the enemy with as little impedimenta as possible, more might have been achieved.

By this arrangement the enemy's forces would have been divided into six parts, instead of into two, in itself an advantage. Each part could not have exceeded in strength more than 1,000 men. Even by this plan the enemy could escape by innumerable roads, but then, unless very large numbers of troops are employed, it is hopeless to endeavour to block all lines of retreat, the force becomes too weak at any one point to deal with the enemy, and it is a thing to be remembered that a column cannot expect help from another part of the force unless they are both advancing along the same path.

General Von Trotha was now chosen to command and a large expeditionary force organised. It was decided that columns were to be made up of so many units with the addition of a few guns. The mounted company was chosen as the tactical unit. It was strong enough when reinforced by a section of artillery to be detached without danger of being cut up, and it was sufficiently mobile to enable it to carry out its marches, for the most part, free of the encumbrance of water-carriers, which a more slowly moving and less widely ranging column would be burdened with. Two or three of these units, with a complement of artillery and machine guns, were considered sufficiently strong to defeat and pursue any force of the enemy encountered. A column could therefore concentrate by units at a desired point with the minimum of trouble. The composition of a mounted company was as follows:

MOUNTED COMPANY.

6 Officers
1 Doctor
1 Veterinary Surgeon

NORTHERN PORTION OF

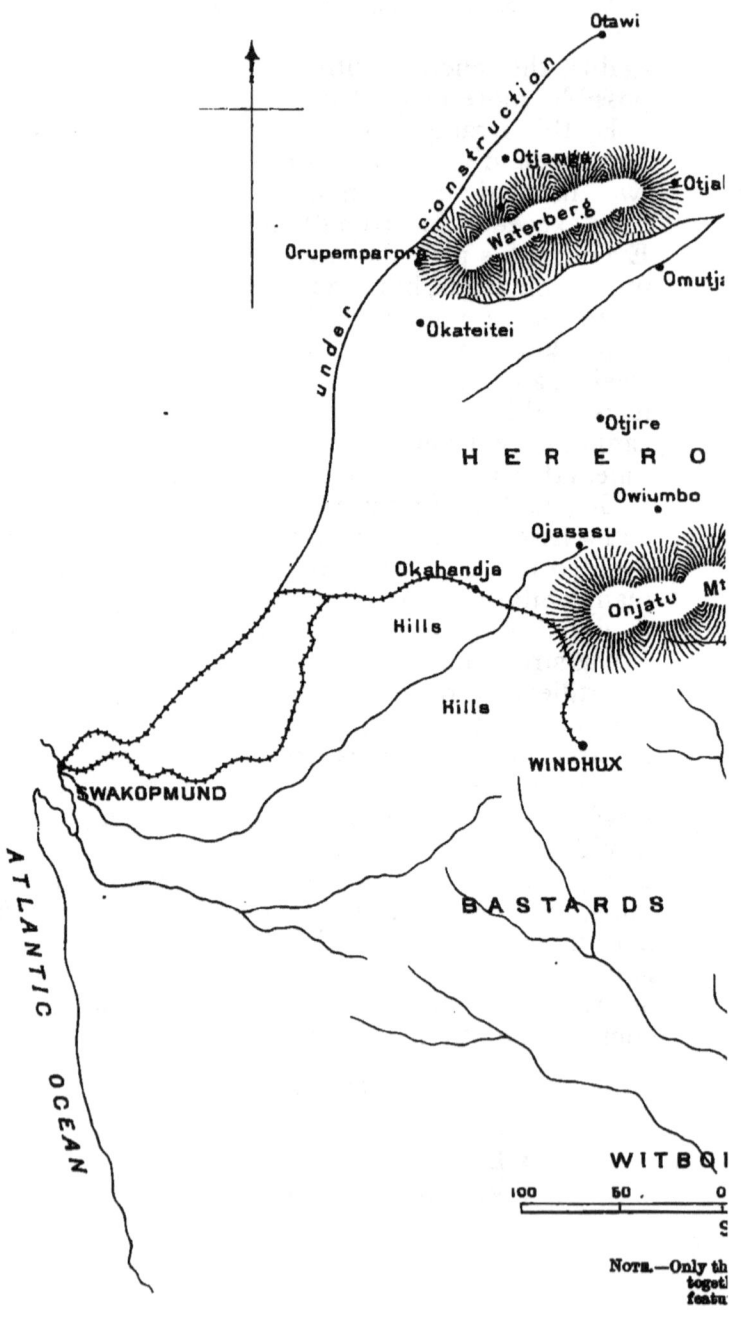

GERMAN S.-W. AFRICA.

Nº 9

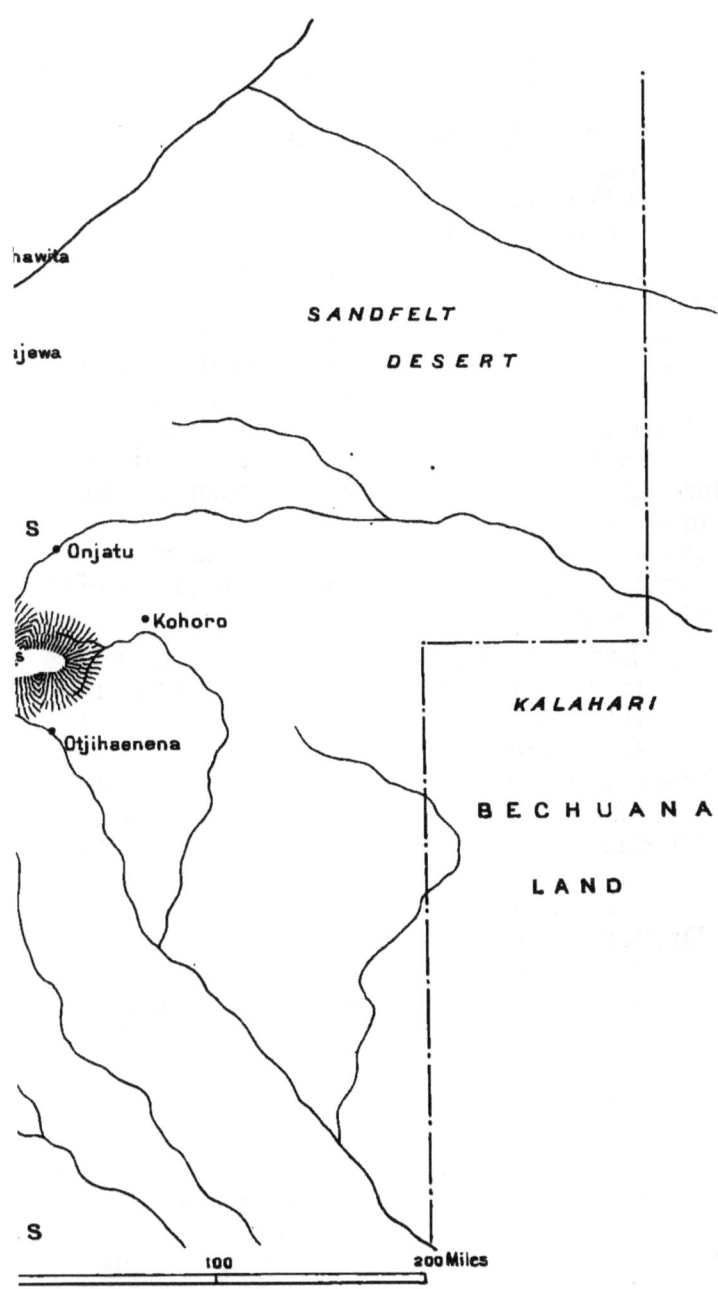

Scale 1" = 90 miles

ose places appearing in the text are shown,
her with a few of the principal posts and
res of the country.

25 Non-Commissioned Officers
152 Men
8 Wagons
30 Native Drivers

The ox-wagon, drawn by 18 to 20 oxen, carries about 4,408 lbs.

One wagon was allowed to every 25 men.

The enemy had meanwhile left the Onjatu Hills and concentrated in the Waterberg to the north.

Von Trotha now formed the troops at his disposal into six detachments, and stationed them round the Waterberg, making a circle of investment, some 235 miles in length.

The commanders and composition of the various detachments, together with their several places of assembly, were as follows :—

> VON ESTORFF—3 companies, 1 battery, detachment of machine guns, or 26 officers, 247 rifles, 4 guns and 4 machine guns, at Otjahewita.
>
> VON DER HEYDE.—3 companies, 2 batteries, or 22 officers, 164 rifles, 8 guns, at Omutjajewa.
>
> MUELLER.—3 companies, 2 batteries, detachment of machine guns, or 20 officers, 219 rifles, 8 guns, en route from Otjira.
>
> DEIMLING.—4 companies, $1\frac{1}{2}$ batteries, or 20 officers, 478 rifles, 6 guns, at Okateitei.
>
> VON FIEDLER.—2 companies, $\frac{1}{2}$ battery, or 4 officers, 180 rifles, 2 guns, at Orupemparora.
>
> VOLKMANN.—1 company, 2 guns, 2 machine guns, or 4 officers, and 200 rifles, at Otjenga.

There were small bodies of Witbois and Bastards attached to some of the columns, but I have taken no account of them.

The dispositions were effected by 3rd August.

Other small detachments were patrolling different parts of the country and guarding the railway from the base. I do not propose to go into the question of their strength and position.

On 7th August reliable reports placed 5,000 to 6,000 of the enemy in the triangle Otjosongombe, Hamakari, Omuweroume. Orders were sent therefore to move forward on 10th August and attack at 6 a.m. 11th August simultaneously.

Mueller and Von der Heyde were given Hamakari as objective, Mueller attacking from the south; Heyde from north-east. Deimling was to move on Omuweroume, and Von Estorff on Waterberg. The last two detachments after reaching their respective places were to co-operate and take he Hereros at Hamakari in flank and rear. Von Fiedler and Volkmann were to bar the line of retreat northwards.

Von Estorff had severe fighting, defeated the enemy, but could not get beyond Otjosongombe that night.

Von der Heyde encountered the enemy $9\frac{1}{2}$ miles north-east of Hamakari, had a hard fight, and ell back for the night to Otjiwarongo.

Mueller fought all day, defeated the enemy, but could not advance past Hamakari that night.

Deimling was weakly opposed, but only reached Waterberg at nightfall.

Von Fiedler and Volkmann occupied the northern outlets to the passes, encountering no resistance.

The following morning the enemy had disappeared, with their cattle, in a south-easterly direction through the gap, nine miles wide, between Mueller and Von der Heyde. The accurate knowledge possessed by the enemy of the smallest paths enabled them to get away. Although no important captures were effected, the Hereros received a

WATERBERG

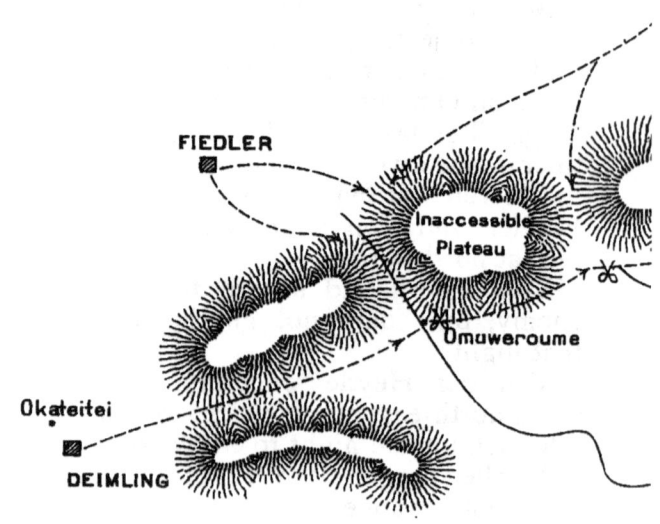

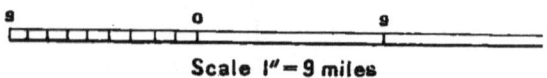

Scale 1" = 9 miles

Hugh Rees, Limited, London.

FIGHT (11·8·1904).

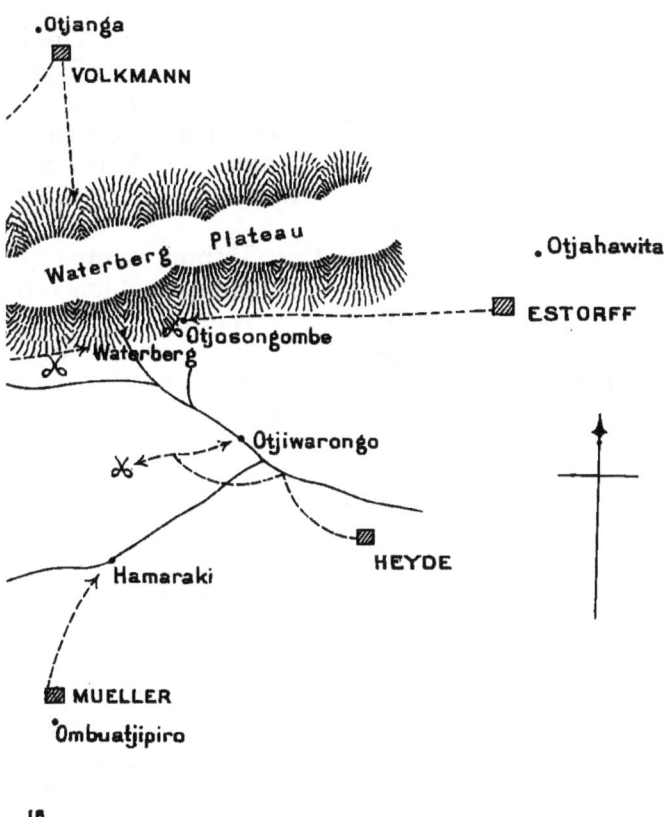

severe blow to their prestige and *moral*. General Von Trotha now followed the enemy, and, pursuing the same surrounding tactics, drove them into the Sand-felt, and there is little doubt but that the insurrection was drawing to a conclusion. Unfortunately, just as the end appeared in view the tribes in the south rose.

By July 31st, 1905, nearly a year later, by which time nearly 16,000 men and 13,000 horses had been sent out to the country, the sum of over £9,000,000 had been voted for the campaign, and the casualties had amounted to something like 4,000 officers and men, the pacification of the country seemed as far off as ever.

Use of Friendlies. There is one point about this German campaign that strikes one, and that is the little use which was made of the friendly tribes, the Witbois and Bastards. With the exception of half a company of the former nation, which was attached to the Von Estorff column, and the same number of the latter tribe, which was with the Mueller detachment during the Waterberg fight, no use, or a very limited one, was made of those people. The German system of Colonial government is of course different from that which is pursued under the Colonial Office in Downing Street. With us a conquered country is handed back, as it were, to its chiefs, and they are allowed, under the superintendence of a white man, to manage affairs ; local institutions and regulations compatible with our ideas of humanity and civilisation remain in force, interior discipline remains, and the chiefs, having an interest in the welfare of their country, and with their power of evil restrained, are at once a hold over the people, and a means by which the white man in charge can reach all and every section and village of the country. These chiefs, in a great many instances, are only too willing to raise levies among their tribes to aid us in our dealings with other tribes, and these levies, although a source of danger as a rule if an attempt is made to use them alongside our troops, owing to their lack of discipline and liability to panic, still, when employed to create a diversion by moving them in the direction of the enemy by different routes to that used by the regular troops, their presence is a distinct advantage. They are also exceedingly useful in blocking avenues of retreat by which the enemy hopes, if beaten, to remove his goods and cattle. Take the Waterberg fight. Had the Germans had a few thousand Witbois and Bastards to lie in ambush on the various paths along which the Hereros escaped, they would probably have succeeded in capturing great numbers of the cattle, and thus adding additional and very severe blows to those already sustained by that tribe during the combat. The levies might be allowed all, or at any rate, a very considerable proportion of the plunder they may be instrumental in capturing, and this inducement is, as a rule, one quite sufficient to promote keenness in the enterprise.

BENIN RIVER EXPEDITION IN 1894.

The following account shows how small a column, judiciously employed, and composed of the right elements, can be counted upon even to overcome the formidable obstacles and carefully prepared stockades bristling with guns, which were a peculiar feature of this expedition.

The chief points of the memorandum issued by Admiral Bedford relating to the attack are as follows :—

General Memorandum.

H.M.S. " Philomel," at Benin
24th Sept., 1894.

1.—The Admiral will, acting with the Consul-General, exercise general supervision and direction of the movements.
2.—Right Attack.—Captain Powell will, on landing, immediately advance to the end of the road, and from there endeavour to get in rear of the guns, and then make his way to the solid ground about Nana's town.
3.—The Admiral and his staff will be with this column along the road.
4.—Left and Centre Attack.—Captain Campbell will establish his guns, &c., in the best position for harassing the enemy, but will not open fire unless they do, or in compliance with orders. He is to be prepared to advance up the main creek as opportunity offers. If possible, definite orders for him to advance will be sent, but in default of these he must act to the best of his judgment.
5.—The stockade is the base, and the wounded are to be sent there. A reserve of water and ammunition will be stored there.
6.—As soon as the creek is open all communication is to be made by it.
7.—The greatest caution is to be exercised when the town is gained to avoid casualties by explosion of small stores of powder which may be scattered about.
8.—Any spirits found to be immediately

SIZE, &c., OF COLUMNS

destroyed. Sentries to be placed on any storehouses.

9.—The men are to be kept carefully in hand, and houses, &c., are not to be set on fire except by order.

The landing will be effected by 5.30 a.m. at the main stockade, the N.C.P. troops and cutters to land outside the stockade below the creek.

RIGHT ATTACK.—In the following order. (See map).

1.—50 N.C.P. troops under Capt. Evenson.
2.—40 road cutters under Mr. Leckie and Mr. Campbell.
3.—17 N.C.P. troops with maxim, Mr. Roupell.
4.—Rocket party, Lieut. Heugh and Sub-Lieut. Hervey.
5.—18 men and maxim, Mr. Staddon, H.M.S. "Phœbe."
6.—37 marines of "Philomel," "Phœbe" and "Widgeon," Sergeant of "Phœbe" in charge.
7.—50 seamen of "Phœbe," Lieut. Hickley and Lieut. Parks.
8.—Ambulance, Staff Surgeon Browne and Dr. Roth, N.C.P.

SUPPORT.—35 seamen of "Widgeon," Lieut. Grant Dalton to remain at bend of road until ordered to advance.

LEFT AND CENTRE ATTACK.—Landing party from "Philomel" with—

Maxim gun, Lieut. Gore-Browne.
7-pounder gun, Lieut. Clarke.
3-pounder gun, Sub-Lieut. Tomlin.
Rockets, Gunner Jennings.

Explosive party, Boatswain Tubb.
Surgeon Maitland.
Engineer Richardson,

will establish themselves in stockade and advance when possible.

Lieut. Marston, of "Widgeon," assisted by Assistant Engineer of "Philomel," to be in charge of base at stockade, under the orders of Captain Campbell.

Fifty carriers will be available to forward stores to the front.

The surgeons of "Widgeon" and "Alecto" will remain to receive the wounded at the stockade.

Staff-Commander Maclean will be in charge of ships, and will be responsible for the firing.

The men are to wear blue and hats; they are to take one day's provisions and 100 rounds of ammunition.

Portable bridges for crossing small creeks to be provided by "Phœbe."

Distinguishing Signals { "Philomel," 3 G's before and after bugle calls. "Widgeon," 2 G's before and after bugle calls.

Details to be arranged by officers in command of columns.

The above was the rough memorandum issued to commanders.

The stockade continually referred to was the large one, about half mile up the creek. This was made the advanced base.

At 4.30 a.m. the N.C.P. troops and cutters landed at the mouth of the creek, at 5.30 a.m. the Right Attack left the stockade, and at 7.45 a.m. the leading troops occupied the south-eastern edge of the town marked H.

The point X on the map was the place where Commander Heugh turned his launch during his reconnaissance, detailed on page 183 in chapter on Reconnaissance.

Luckily he did so, for the battery opened fire, expecting he was going to retire. Had he proceeded up the creek, turned the bend, and come alongside the main battery facing west, not a man of the party could have escaped.

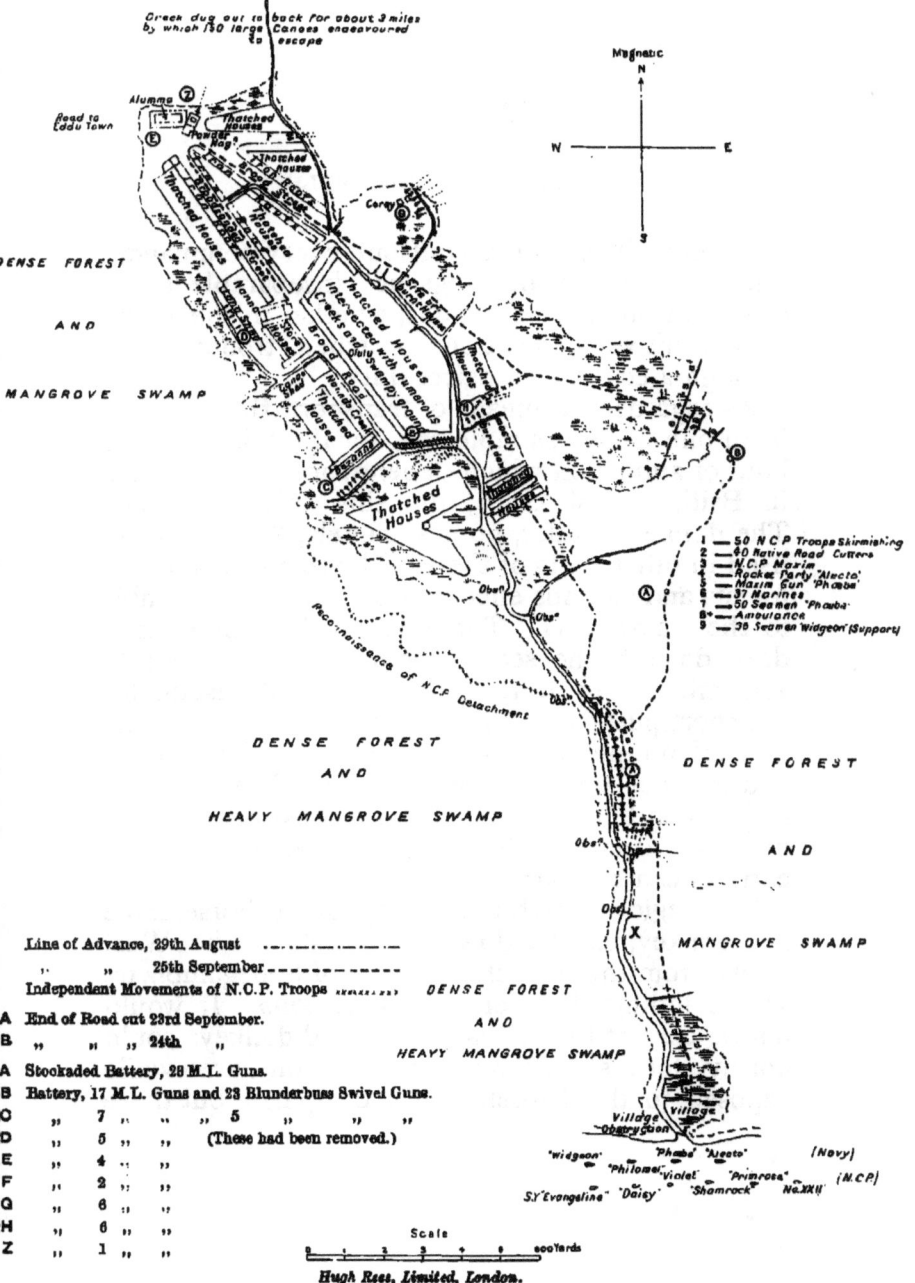

CHAPTER III.

TRANSPORT AND SUPPLIES.

THE difficulties which confront every commander under these two headings are inseparable to all classes of military operations, whether in the nature of a punitive expedition, or when troops move through a country on patrol duty.

As regards the means of transport, this question is, in one sense, a simple one, for there is only one kind of animal on which dependence can be placed in British West Africa, and this animal is man. The donkeys, mules, ponies, camels, &c., which are used in other parts of the world are useless in the forests and swamps encountered from the Gambia to the Cameroons. The forest belt, coming as it does, down to the sea, varies in width from 200 to 400 miles. In it four-footed animals useful for transport purposes will not live. As one goes further inland, ponies exist, but only in small numbers, and it is not until one arrives in the French territory which bounds our African possessions on their northern frontier that anything except human carriers can be counted upon.

The regions which are deadly for the horse, mule and donkey, extend down the whole of the West Coast, from the French province of Senegambia to, and including, the German Cameroons. It would not be correct to say that ponies and donkeys could not live for a short time in these regions, even while exposed to the hardships of a campaign, but there

TRANSPORT AND SUPPLIES 87

does not seem to be any object in trying them; there is no grazing country for them, all fodder would have to be carried, and they would be exceedingly costly as compared with the carrier. Carts also, even of the Indian ekka type, would be quite unsuitable and impossible in the present condition of the native bush paths.

In German South-West Africa, however, it seems to be quite another matter. The coast line there is low and with scarcely any indentations, Walfish Bay, which belongs to us, being the only one of note in a length of over 900 miles. Inland, however, the country is quite different from our fever laden forests, lying, as they do, on the monotonous level. A range of high plateaux runs north and south, roughly parallel to the sea, the whole length of the colony. This range is separated from the sea by a waterless and sterile tract of land varying in width from 45 to 90 miles, but once in the hills, a comparatively healthy and the most populous part of the country is found. The pasturages of part of these regions are such that the Hereros, a warlike shepherd tribe, have swept down from the north and have overrun them.

The Germans, therefore, in their campaign for the subjugation of these people, were able to employ mules and horses, not only for transport, but for mounting companies of infantry and for their guns.

Up to the end of the first quarter of 1904, 647 horses and 733 mules were purchased in Argentina, and 1,310 horses and 420 mules were bought at the Cape. By the 31st July, 1905, something like 13,000 horses had been imported into the country. There was great difficulty in landing them on the inhospitable coast, but when once on shore, they appear to do well. We who are accustomed to deal with the question of buying, shipping, disembarking, and organizing a mass of animals, bought in a country far from the scene of operations, know well the difficulties which must be expected to crop up, and can, to a great extent, minimise the trouble. The Germans, however, were new to the work. Operations had to be delayed while the half savage animals were broken in, not only to the saddle, but to harness. The French official account of this campaign very truly states : "A number (X) of men drawn from all arms, and a number (Y) of horses not broken into the saddle or for draught do not suffice to constitute a company, and *a fortiori*, a battery, ready to go on service."

East Coast of Africa. On the East Coast of Africa carriers have been used, for the most part, for transport work, but the country is more suitable for grazing than is the West Coast, and therefore, should it be found necessary, there seems to be no reason why four-footed transport animals should not be tried in perhaps some large expedition of the future.

Somaliland. In Somaliland, all and every kind of transport was brought into requisition, ponies, carriers, camels, and even the Indian ekka, all taking their places along the lines of communications between Berbera, Upper Sheikh and the interior depots, Bohotle and Damot, a total distance of 255 miles.

A large number of Indian and Arab coolies from Aden were employed at the base at Berbera for the work of unloading ships, &c. There were two Army Service Corps companies, under Captains Watling and Scott, sent from South Africa, and these worked the line from Berbera to Lower Sheikh. Each company consisted of 40 mule wagons and 450 mules, with the proper complement of Army Service Corps men, civilian conductors and native drivers. Although they managed fairly

TRANSPORT AND SUPPLIES

well, the country was hardly suited for this kind of transport. Some type of cart with broad tyred wheels would have been better, perhaps, owing to the deep sand.

At Lower Sheikh the Army Service Corps handed the stores over to a transit depot, and they were conveyed up the Sheikh Pass to Upper Sheikh at the top by the Indian pack mule train. From here the camel corps conveyed them on to the front. At Upper Sheikh were three trains of ekkas which came from India, and also some camel carts. Convoys often came right down to the base and returned to the front with stores, but as a rule the stage system was employed and worked well. This is the general system employed in India. It consists in making posts from 10 to 12 miles apart, at which are stationed a detachment of the transport corps. The transport from each post carries stores on to the next and returns, having dropped them.

As carriers, however, are the principal means of transport in the bush, their use and numbers will be entered into in some detail. These carriers are capable of marching, on the average, about 15 miles a day with a load of from 50 to 70 lbs. on their heads. It has been found that good men can be relied upon to carry 70 lbs., but for the average man 50 lbs. is quite enough, and if loads are limited to this latter weight, fewer carriers will break down, and consequently work will be apt to be conducted with greater regularity and certainty. The ·303 S.A.A. box, containing 840 cartridges, weighs just 60 lbs., and it has been found that the ammunition carrier seldom breaks down, whereas men carrying other loads ranging up to 70 lbs. have often to be changed and numbers augmented to allow of reliefs. This box, being such a compact load, is much easier to carry and to balance on the head

Carriers.

than a much lighter load with a more easily changed centre of gravity. A great many men pooh-pooh the idea of only a 50 lb. load, but be it remembered that in this, as in most other cases, "the more haste the less speed," and that a column of heavily-laden carriers with frequent breakdowns is a source of considerable annoyance, delay and fatigue, not only to the officers in charge, but to the other carriers themselves, who are kept waiting while the breakdown is rectified.

The Mendi and Timini from Sierra Leone, and the Hausa and up country Yoruba, are certainly the best of the West Coast tribes as far as stamina goes, and perhaps their loads might be raised to 60 or even 70 lbs., but a commander cannot always get the whole of his carriers from these tribes, and therefore loads should be kept as nearly as possible to 50 lbs. For Sir J. Willcocks' expedition in Ashanti, the Sierra Leone men were found to be the best, but some four thousand five hundred excellent men came from the East of Africa, from Zanzibar and Mombassa.

Now with reference to the numbers of carriers required. Expeditions vary greatly as regards the numbers of troops employed and the number of columns co-operating. Take the small expedition under 500 of all ranks.

Say it is composed as under :—

15 officers, 5 European N.C.O.'s.

3 Companies } of 130 R. & F. each... 390 Natives.
3 Maxims

1 75-millimetre gun, 12 gunners ... 12 ,,

Carriers for millimetre (trained) ... 62 ,,

                                                                    464

of which 402 are fighting men.

TRANSPORT AND SUPPLIES

These small expeditions, be they punitive or otherwise, are as a rule able to subsist on the country, and food need only be taken for the Europeans. The yams, kokos, bananas, plaintains, &c., of which there are large stores in every country, will be amply sufficient to feed the force, and this eating-up of the enemy's supplies is one of our chief weapons, and is sure eventually to bring the most obstinate to terms.

Truculent chiefs whose power is in the number of their fighting men soon lose their followers when hunger begins to be felt, and the large stores of food in the country have been found and stacked in the main camp of the white man.

Carriers for the above force would be as follows:—

One carrier is supplied to every 10 soldiers to carry their odds and ends of kit. The men of the West African Frontier Force want little in the way of transport. They like to carry a few cleaning materials for their carbines, and each man takes a change of clothes, and perhaps a spare pair of chuplies or light shoes. Waterproof bags are supplied to carry the changes for 10 men, and these bags, if properly packed, should not weigh more than 55 lbs. at most. Careful supervision by section commanders and company officers of the packing of these bags is required; men try to get all their worldly goods, irrespective of weight, into them. One morning, the day after the capture of a town, a carrier was seen endeavouring to lift the kit bag, which was his load, with indifferent success. On opening it, the contents seemed to consist of little else but bundles of brass rods which had been looted the day before. Needless to say, these had to go, much to the chagrin of their possessor.

Soldiers' Kits.

Maxims.   Each maxim is allowed five carriers, one for the gun, one for the tripod, and three for the ammunition; each carrier can carry three belts, each containing 250 rounds. Therefore the three carriers can carry 2,250 rounds. Belts when expended can be reloaded each day from the reserve ammunition.

Guns.   The Vickers-Maxim quick-firing gun of 75-millimetre calibre requires 32 carriers for the gun and carriage, and 30 more are necessary for a fair proportion of ammunition. These men, however, are not ordinary carriers, but are specially enlisted and are of good physique and recognised pluck. Most of them are splendid men, and it is often a fine sight to see them struggling with desperate energy under their great loads through swamps and awkward places, utterly regardless of the enemy's fire, so that they may, as quickly as possible, bring the several parts of the gun to a good position, and there hand over to the gunners, who, in almost less time than it takes to write, have mounted the gun and come into action. No half-hearted men of even ordinary strength and stature could be entrusted with the job.

The following shows the weight of the gun and its various parts, together with the distribution of the gun detachment and the 32 carriers to the loads in the "order of march":—

ORDER OF MARCH OF 2·95IN. OR 75 M/M GUN DISMOUNTED.

	1. 2. 3.	Trail.	Axle. 4	Wheels.	Jacket.	Gun.	6. 7. 5. 10. 11. 12.
Direction of Advance.			8	9			
	Carriers 8		1	1	1	8	8
	Weight in lbs. 228		48	68	68	196	236

This provides a relief of four carriers for the trail, jacket and gun.

TRANSPORT AND SUPPLIES 93

It will be seen that each of the trail carriers has a load of something over 57 lbs. and those of the gun over 59 lbs. each, when the weight is taken evenly amongst the four men.

In the case of the 7-pounder gun, fewer carriers are required, and these need not be highly trained. Twelve carriers are sufficient for the gun, and ten more are necessary for the ammunition.

It will be seen that as regards length of column and number of mouths to feed, one 75-millimetre gun is equal to about three 7-pounders. This is a good ratio also as regards the power of each gun. It is generally considered that the 75-millimetre is worth three of the smaller guns.

The question of the carriers for the white men of the column is a matter for consideration, and depends nearly altogether on the time the column remains a flying one and is out of touch with the base. Taking the Ibeku-Olokoro Expedition as a fair sample of small punitive work. The expedition rendezvoused at Bendi, in Southern Nigeria, on October 24th, 1902, which place was about three miles from the enemy's frontier. Stores and ammunition for the Europeans and natives had been collected in Bendi, and it served as the base, being well garrisoned and within easy and safe communication of Arochuku, and thence to Old Calabar. *[Supplies and Carriers for Europeans.]*

It was reckoned that the column might be cut off for perhaps three weeks from the base. Each European was therefore allowed six personal carriers, distributed as under, one for bedding, one for clothes, three for food and drink, and one for water.

The commanding officer had eight, the two extra being used for his office box, stationery, &c.

"Chop" boxes containing one week's food and drink were made up as under, and are a carrier's load.

Quantity.	Description.
7 lbs.	meat (tinned).
5 lbs.	of wheatmeal biscuits or 6 lbs. of flour (alternative).
2 lbs.	fancy biscuits.
4 tins	Ideal milk.
2 tins	of jam or marmalade.
½ lb.	of tinned butter.
½ lb.	tea, coffee or cocoa.
⅛ bottle	Worcestershire sauce.
3 tins	pea soup.
4 ozs.	of salt.
7 lbs.	of rice.
2 lbs.	of sugar.
4 ozs.	of currie powder.
1 bottle	of whiskey.
1 bottle	of gin.
1 lb.	vegetables (compressed).

These were used with success on the Ashanti (1900) and Aro Expeditions. The boxes themselves should be strong and fitted with a padlock. When empty they can be sent to the base and replenished. The boxes will be found of great convenience should it be necessary to detach a party for reconnoitring or other purposes. Each European can take a "chop" box, or one may be allowed to every two white men, as suggested by Colonel Montanaro in his pamphlet on bush fighting.

For the Benin Expedition in 1897, commanded by Sir Harry Rawson, K.C.B., ration boxes were made up so as to contain rations for 24 men for 24 hours. These applied only, however, to the sailors and marines landed from the ships. Each box weighed 56 lbs., and was complete in every detail, even to candles and matches for the day.

TRANSPORT AND SUPPLIES

A box contained

Biscuit	12 lbs.
Preserved Meat	12 ,,
Sugar	3 ,,
Chocolate	1½ ,,
Tea	⅝ ,,
Coffee	1½ ,,
Sugar	¾ ,,

Salt, pepper, mustard, curry powder, candles and two boxes of matches.

The above rations were found sufficient for white men who were landed from ships for two or three weeks only, but would not be on a generous enough scale for those living on the coast, who perhaps would have to be in the bush and on the march for six months or more.

It is a good scale, however, for white troops for a short expedition. It will be gathered from this how impossible it would be to carry on a lengthy expedition in West Africa in which any large numbers of white troops were employed. The carrier columns would become enormous.

Some few details of Sir Garnet Wolseley's expedition in Ashanti in 1873 may be of interest to show what has been done with white troops in this pestilential climate, and how their employment adds enormously to the difficulties of a commander.

The daily ration for each white soldier during this campaign was :— *

BREAD.—1½ lbs. of fresh bread or 1¼ lbs. of biscuit, or 1 lb. flour.

MEAT.—1½ lbs. fresh or salted meat, or 1 lb. preserved meat.

* "The Soldier's Pocket Book," by Sir Garnet Wolseley.

VEGETABLES.—2 ozs. rice or peas, or 4 ozs. preserved potatoes, or 1 lb. fresh vegetables.

Tea, ¾ oz. Salt, ½ oz. Sugar, 3 ozs. Pepper, 1-36 oz. 4 ozs. sausage was issued as well when engagements or long marches were anticipated.

A British battalion of 650 men required 650 carriers, exclusive of rations, as follows :—

650 soldiers, one carrier to every three for kit	217 carriers
30 officers' baggage	30 ,,
Officers' cooking pots	10 ,,
82 camp kettles, 9 kettles per carrier	9 ,,
Ammunition	70 ,,
Orderly room, &c.	2 ,,
40 cots, 6 carriers per cot	240 ,,
Medical officer's orderlies	6 ,,
Head men, 28 ; 6 per cent. spare 38	66 ,,
Total	650 carriers.

From 35 to 40 carriers more would be needed to carry the daily rations for these 650 men, not to mention the officers. Ten days flying column would therefore add some 400 carriers to the column, bringing the numbers to about 1,050. Attach a few guns to this battalion, and before the column is ready to move off the carriers will be close on 1,300 or 1,400 in number, for in the above calculations no medical stores or comforts have been reckoned with. In fact, generally speaking, a European force detached for a week or 10 days as a flying column will require twice as many carriers at least as a force composed of native troops. The base supplies and accommodation, carriers required for the lines of communication, size and accommodation of advanced depots, hospitals, &c., will consequently all be on a much more extensive scale

TRANSPORT AND SUPPLIES

for European troops, and will thus add greatly to the expense of the campaign. The difficulties of organization and responsibilities of a commander will be correspondingly increased.

For peaceful patrols as well as for expeditionary work, boxes containing food and drink for one European for one week can be ordered at the Army and Navy Stores. These boxes should be strong, and with a padlock inside, so that when the box is unscrewed it can be fitted with it and kept locked. The box and contents should not weigh more than 55 lbs., and should not cost, carriage and all from England, more than 35s. An officer is allowed 5s. per diem when away from his station on "bush" work, and this allowance will pay for the boxes easily.

European Food for One Week.

Two or three different kinds of boxes might be ordered, each containing different food, so that a change of diet, which is so beneficial, would be possible. Say three different kinds were made up painted A, B and C on the outside. Instructions left at home that on receipt of a cable saying so many dozen of each were required, they could be despatched almost at once.

The following is a sample box, and would be found none too luxurious for a deadly climate, in which a European ought to do himself "well" to keep fit.

MEAT—   PRICE.

	£	s.	d.
½ tin beef a la mode	0	0	11
½ tin beef a la jardinière	0	0	11
½ tin veal and green peas	0	1	1
½ tin calf's tongue and tomato	0	1	1
½ tin curried fowl	0	0	11½
½ tin Oxford sausages	0	0	9
1 tin sliced bacon	0	1	0½
2 tins potted meat	0	1	0
Carried forward	0	7	9

		£	s.	d.	£	s.	d.
	Brought forward				0	7	9
FISH—		PRICE.					
	6 tins sardines in oil (small)	0	2	5			
					0	2	5
BREAD OR BISCUITS—							
	7 lb. tin cabin biscuits	0	2	0			
	1 lb. tin Petit Beurre biscuits	0	0	10			
					0	2	10
FRUIT AND JAM—							
	1 tin apricots in syrup	0	0	10½			
	1 "lever lid" tin containing ¾ lb. French plums and ½ figs	0	1	0			
	6. ¼ tins jam	0	0	10			
					0	2	8½
TEA, &C.—							
	¼ cutter tin tea	0	0	7½			
	¼ cutter tin coffee	0	0	6½			
	½ tin chocolate food	0	0	10½			
					0	2	0½
SUGAR—							
	1 lb. cutter tin granulated sugar	0	0	4			
	1 bottle saccharine	0	0	8			
					0	1	0
MILK—							
	4. ½ tins Ideal milk	0	0	11			
					0	0	11
BUTTER, &C.—							
	½ tin Esbensen's butter	0	0	11½			
	½ tin lard	0	0	5			
	1 jar Imperial cheese	0	0	11			
					0	2	3½
RICE, &C.—							
	1 lb tin rice (cutter lid)	0	0	4			
	1 lb. tin rolled breakfast oats	0	0	4½			
	2 small plum puddings	0	1	0			
					0	1	8½
VEGETABLES—							
	1 tin haricot beans	0	0	4			
	1 tin dried onions	0	0	3½			
	1 tin dried Julienne	0	0	3½			
					0	0	11½
	Carried forward				£1	4	7½

		£	s.	d.
Brought forward		1	4	7½

LIME JUICE— PRICE.

	£	s.	d.
1 bottle (cordial if preferred)	0	0	5½
	0	0	5½

SOUP—

	£	s.	d.
6 tins pea, Scotch broth and Mulligatawny	0	0	10½
	0	0	10½

SUNDRIES—

	£	s.	d.
½ tin salt...	0	0	2
1 oz. mustard...	0	0	1
1 oz. pepper	0	0	2
6 candles	0	0	4½
1 bottle Worcester sauce	0	0	9
1 tin dubbin	0	0	1
¼ bar carbolic soap	0	0	2
1 tin opener	0	0	1½
1 packet toilet paper	0	0	4
Matches	0	0	2
Venesta case fitted with padlock... ...	0	3	0
	0	5	5
	£1	11	4

A total of 31s. 4d., leaving nearly 4s. per case for carriage out.

This is an elaborate box, but none too much for a week's hard work in the bush. Some of the items might be cut out, and a bottle of whisky and gin added in their place; but even left as it is, and the liquor added, the expense to a man for one week's good food and drink could not be called heavy.

With regard to the native troops and their rations, they can in most cases subsist on the country, but it may be necessary to carry rice for them. Each native soldier receives 1½lbs. as a daily ration. Carriers, 1lb. Therefore a 56lb. bag of rice will be required daily for 36 soldiers, or 56 carriers. It is advisable, in making these calculations, to allow for waste. Branches of

For Natives' Food.

trees rip bags, and careless or tired carriers soon damage their loads. It is often found that at the end of a week's march bags of rice are as much as 5lb. and 6lb. under weight. When living on the country, two good yams are a sufficient ration for the soldiers—they supplement these with country peppers, herbs, odds and ends of fruit, vegetables, and palm oil. When bullocks and goats are captured, meat can be served out. It is an easy matter to feed a column of 450 native soldiers, with its complement of carriers, in almost any country in West Africa, for a month or six weeks. The natives of the country stack their yams, when the harvest is gathered, in enormous enclosures. Lines of light framework are erected, about 6ft. high, and in some cases over half a mile long. Each yam is put into a "pigeon-hole" in this structure, and there remains until eaten or bartered in the markets. In some countries these enclosures hold as many as half a million yams, in perfect condition.

The principal meal of all natives is in the evening, when they roast their yams in the embers of a fire, beat them into "foo foo," and add peppers, etc., and palm oil, to taste. They put any bits left over into their haversacks, to help them through the next day, but really do not seem to want a square meal again until the evening.

Although the West Coast native can live on rice for a short time, and it is an excellent supplement to any ration which may be gathered for him, still, it is not his regular food, and at times when yams have been scarce, and the rice ration has been the only one available, dysentery has resulted. The Krooboy, of course, can, and does, thrive on rice. He has become used to it, owing to his work in factories, and also to his voyages on the West Coast

TRANSPORT AND SUPPLIES

steamers; but this is the only race which can thrive on this form of food.

These "boys," however, are impossible to get for transport purposes, owing to the restrictions imposed by the Liberian Government on the number of Kroomen who may leave their country annually. Their peculiarities of diet, therefore, need not be taken into account.

The hospital carriers are always a difficult matter to arrange for. The medical officer, quite rightly, wants all he can get (so does everybody else for that matter), and it is essential that his number be as large as is consistent with safety, but every extra man means another mouth to feed and another two or three yards of path to guard in action, and so the number must be cut down to the minimum. Hospital.

A fairly good rule for such columns is to give him one carrier for every nine fighting men of the force employed. Before fighting begins he will of course have a lot of spare men : these should on no account be used to carry odds and ends for people. Once in action, and the hammocks and stretchers are got ready, every man will most probably be needed for his legitimate work.

Colonel Montanaro in his "Hints for a Bush Campaign," lays down the number 300 as required for a force of 60 Europeans and 1,200 rank and file. This is in the proportion of one carrier to every four fighting men, and is a very high percentage; still, with six carriers to each hammock it cannot be called by any means an excessive number. Supposing the cases of instruments, boxes of drugs, medicines and dressings, not to mention medical comforts, and water jars with sterilized water, required 30 carriers, it would leave 270 men for hammock work, enough for 45 hammocks only;

should severe opposition be encountered this would only allow for under 4 per cent. of the column being so severely wounded as to necessitate their being carried, certainly a small enough percentage. It must be remembered also that all dead must be carried out of action; mutilation at least, and probably a cannibal feast by the enemy, follows the abandonment of any dead soldier on the scene of the conflict.

As a rule, then, the number of carriers for medical work will not vary directly, as the size of the force; the percentage will be greater for a larger than for a smaller number of combatants.

The numbers, of course, again depend to a great extent on the amount of opposition to be expected. Against Ashantis well armed a greater number will be required than against inferior and poorly armed races.

Should we ever have to contend against the native forces of another European power as well armed as ourselves, and this is not at all an improbable contingency one of these days, the medical carrier column will be larger than ever.

Of course, should rice be carried for the forces, a certain number of these carriers will become free each day as the food is consumed, and these can all go to the medical officer; also the two relief men for each hammock can be made to aid in carrying other hammocks, but only for a comparatively short distance, and they should never be counted on. Plenty of spare hammocks should be carried, rolled up, and without the pole weigh next to nothing.

Unless a regular bearer company has been formed in peace time, the first duty of a medical officer attached to a column is to form and train one. This will not take long. Either ordinary carriers

TRANSPORT AND SUPPLIES 103

or soldiers should be taken for this work. Two stretchers per company are sufficient, each manned by two men, who are soon taught how to open out and close a stretcher, as well as the proper way to lift up a wounded man and place him on it.

Ammunition carriers for the guns have been dealt with; for the S.A.A. the numbers depend on the length of time the column is expected to be a flying one, the temper of the enemy and amount of resistance anticipated, and also to a great extent whether the troops composing the column are proved men possessing good fire discipline, or are untried, and therefore at first likely to be wasteful. *S. A. Ammunition.*

Each soldier carries 100 rounds to start with, so the question is, how many rounds per man in reserve should be carried? Commanders of course differ on this all-important question, and it is naturally impossible to gauge beforehand the exact amount required. Experience has taught that for expeditions against most of the tribes to be met with in British West Africa a reserve of 150 rounds per rifle is ample, provided the force consists of 350 to 500 men, and the column is not out of touch with the advanced depot or base for more than three weeks. Suppose the force is, as above, 500 men, the reserve will be 75,000 or a total of 125,000 rounds. This amount is generally ample for most expeditions in West Africa provided the troops are good. Colonel Montanaro says 200 rounds per rifle in reserve for a force of 1,200 men. This would give a total of 360,000 rounds with the column, an exceedingly large quantity, even for Ashanti land, where the enemy was well armed and fought with great determination; still it is better to have too many rounds than too few, and one would like to carry 500 rounds per man were it not for the old question cropping up of food and protection for every carrier.

The number of rounds should vary inversely as the number of troops employed—*i.e.*, a smaller force should carry a larger number of rounds per rifle in reserve than a larger force. The small force is more likely to get into trouble and be surrounded, and will, therefore, probably require them. It might be dangerous to send off a company for three weeks' punitive work unless it had a reserve of 250 rounds per man.

There ought never to be less than a further 200 to 300 rounds per rifle at the advanced depôt, or base, on which the troops can at once depend.

During the Aro Expedition the total S.A.A. expended amounted to only 40,732 rounds, or under 23 rounds per man of the fighting force.*

This is very remarkable in face of the fighting and opposition encountered.

Colonel Montanaro, in his final despatch, attributes this small expenditure to "the present system of scouting, as commanders of columns were able to make a free use of the bayonet by outflanking and rushing the enemy's positions. This was found to be infinitely more effective than firing into the thick bush on an unseen enemy, and certainly economised the ammunition, and enabled me to make a reduction of 50 per cent. in the amount of reserve ammunition carried by each column."

In the Ibeku-Olokoro Expedition, towards the end of 1902, 226 rank and file fired 11,134 rounds S.A.A. in 54 days, or an average of just under 50 rounds per man.

Four expeditions have been selected out of the twelve or thirteen carried out in the Nigerias during

*A.F.F. despatches, "London Gazette," Sept., 1902.

TRANSPORT AND SUPPLIES 105

the dry season 1903-4, and the amount of ammunition expended in them is interesting, and shows a fire discipline of a high order.*

In the Mkpani country (September, 1903), Major A. M. N. Mackenzie commanded a column, and the rank and file numbered 288. 11,680 rounds S.A.A. were expended, or about 41 per man, in the fighting, which lasted for five days.

Colonel Montanaro commanded a force which operated in the Ibibio country, starting in January, 1904. The duration was some two and a half months. 428 rank and file fired 15,103 rounds, or about 36 per man.

On 17th January, 1904, Major Hogg, 4th Hussars, organised an expedition for operations in the Asaba hinterland. The resistance lasted about three months. 305 rank and file expended 11,522 rounds, or an average of about 38 rounds per man.

To punish the murderers of Captain O'Riordan and Mr. Amyatt-Burney in the Bassa country, Major Merrick commanded 262 men, and in January, 1904, in seven days' severe fighting, 8,263 rounds were fired, or about 40 per carbine. The operations lasted just three months in all, and during that time under 75 rounds per man were fired.

A system by which section reserve ammunition is carried has been found to work well.

Two boxes S.A.A. per section (which gives about 64 rounds extra per man), taken from the general reserve, are carried by specially selected, strong, and courageous carriers. These two men should sleep and live with their section in camp and on the march, and should follow it everywhere in action. The men are proud of being treated as soldiers, and soon become imbued with a high spirit of *esprit de corps*.

These boxes should never be opened except in

*Despatches, " London Gazette," August, 1905.

action in case of a shortage of ammunition; the soldier's 100 rounds should be replenished at the end of the day from the general reserve.

Apart from the advantage of this method under which a section can be at once detached from the column and sent off on a special mission, it tends to decrease the long carrier column, the protection of which is a constant source of anxiety to a commander. There are objections to this method undoubtedly; say, for instance, one carrier is shot, one of the soldiers has to carry the box until another carrier can be found. It has been found to work well, however, in several expeditions.

Tents. There remain now only tents for the white men, and water jars to complete the column.

The former are not imperative, and for any large expedition in which numbers of white men are engaged, they are out of the question, owing to the numbers of carriers required for their transport. There can be no doubt, however, that their use is decidedly advantageous, and men keep their health better when under cover; but then again, it is possible for an expedition to be carried to a successful conclusion without tents. They must be looked upon therefore as a luxury. They can be taken on small columns with perhaps twelve to fifteen white men all told, and will be found very comforting should the season be rainy.

A large square single fly (12ft. by 8ft. wide, when pitched) with front and back doors which lace up the middle, are the most useful. Three beds can be put in these, and it is fairly comfortable. With only two beds it is luxury. Six of these tents will accommodate sixteen white men: the commanding officer and his staff officer in one, the political officer and medical officer in another, and the remainder, three in a tent. Twenty-four carriers

TRANSPORT AND SUPPLIES 107

are, however, needed, and they take up a lot of room on the line of march.

With regard to the water jars, these are by no means a luxury, but a dire necessity. *Water.*

They are made of aluminium protected by basket work, and have a felt pad underneath to save the carrier's head. Each holds $5\frac{1}{4}$ gallons, and weighs when full about 55lbs. Each white man should have one. It is a good plan for two men to go shares, using the contents of one jar, while the other is being cleaned and refilled. Besides the one for each white man, a certain number are given to the hospital, and the boiled and filtered water is used for washing and dressing wounds.

Therefore for the column detailed above, the following carriers would be required for three weeks' work :— *Example.*

1 Commanding Officer	8
1 Staff Officer ...	6
1 Political Officer ...	6
1 Medical Officer ...	6
1 Artillery Officer ...	6
9 Company Officers ...	54
4 European N.C.O's., including one for Medical Officer ...	24
1 Officer & 1 European N.C.O. in charge of Carriers	12
3 Companies, about 390 R. & F., kits ...	39
1 2·95in. gun, 12 gunners, kits ...	2
Reserve ammunition 150 rounds per carbine=58,500 rounds	70
Hospital, about ...	45

Spare Carriers, 10 per cent. ...	...	28
Head men ...	...	13

Total 319

It is seldom that so many Europeans as are enumerated above will be available per company, owing to men on leave and on the sick list. In the above list, the regularly enlisted gun carriers have not been included. These amount to 62 men. Should the number be not available, the balance must be made up of ordinary carriers, and of course these will augment the total arrived at above.

To allow for casualties from every cause, 10 per cent. spare carriers should be taken. Lastly, carrier head men are required, one to every twenty to twenty-five men.

Northern Nigeria. The country of Northern Nigeria is much more varied than in the other colonies of West Africa. There is no forest to speak of, and the bush is not nearly so dense as in Sierra Leone or Southern Nigeria. Except in the north, troops on the march are confined to single file, as in the forest countries, and up to the present, carriers have been the means of transport. As regards food and supplies, the country is far less fertile than in Southern Nigeria, Lagos and the other colonies bordering on the sea, and several days' reserve supplies for natives have, except in certain seasons of the year, and in certain areas, to be carried by the troops. The question of water is also a serious factor, and for five or six months in the year a general scarcity of this precious fluid affects operations and the length of marches. At the height of the dry season, in March and April, its scarcity causes great difficulties, and entails sometimes very long marches. The carrier

TRANSPORT AND SUPPLIES

column, where single file is imperative, is protected as in bush countries. Where the country is open and square formations are adopted, the carriers are protected by being inside the square. There are reasons against adopting this method of protecting transport if it can be avoided. Should a side of the square be heavily attacked and temporary confusion ensue, carriers, and more so, transport animals, are inclined to rush to the safe side, or bolt altogether, and so upset all formations and render a dangerous situation worse. There can be no doubt that the loss and disaster which our arms sustained at Erego in Somaliland was due to the stampede of the transport animals. *Erego, Somaliland.*

The force was attacked on all sides in a very thick bush, and at once formed three sides of a square, enclosed the baggage animals and water transport, the rear being closed by three companies. On the left, owing to the fierceness of the attack, and also to the fact that the troops consisted of for the most part recently raised levies, the face was driven in, and the stampeding animals made things worse. The enemy was eventually repulsed, but some thousand camels with water-tins and ammunition boxes rushed away into the jungle, scattering their loads everywhere.

The casualties were very severe, and although the enemy lost heavily, all plans had to be re-considered, owing to the fact that many camels had been shot, and the transport seriously disorganised.

It would be impossible of course to march and fight with the transport inside a square were the enemy in possession of long-range firearms and light guns. The mark presented by this disposition would be too conspicuous.

When a serious attack is expected, in every class of fighting and in most situations it is generally *Dividing a Force.*

possible to leave the bulk of the carriers with an escort in a secure position, such as a walled village, or behind a river, and then with a purely fighting force, unhampered, meet the enemy.

Enlisting Carriers. It is needless to point out that when enlisting carriers for a campaign a very strict medical examination of each man is necessary, All men with blemishes which might detract from their powers of endurance should be cast. Hard work, exposure, and frequently short rations is the daily round of a carrier's life, and, therefore, no weaklings, or men liable to break down when the strain comes, are of any use. Having selected them, have them vaccinated. Small-pox once amongst the carriers is difficult to stamp out, and its presence seriously interrupts the conduct of a campaign.

Two Classes of Transport. In most expeditions the transport can be divided into two classes, (*a*) that with the troops actually in touch with the enemy, and (*b*) that along the lines of communication conveying stores, etc., from the base to the advanced depôts. The arrangement and numbers of carriers required with the columns has been discussed; it now remains to touch on the system by which the gangs of carriers employed along the line of communication are organised. The country through which the stores have to be carried is very often outside the danger zone; but even so, a certain proportion of troops should be allotted to the various halting places for police duty. A guard should always accompany every gang of carriers to prevent pilfering of the stores, and the desertion now and then of men who have become tired of the work. They are useful, also, to keep the gangs up to scheduled time. Work is simplified at the depôts if the arrival and departure of the gangs are at fixed hours.

TRANSPORT AND SUPPLIES

The carriers on enlistment should be told off into corps of 500 men each. It is advisable to have at least one British officer, one British non-commissioned officer, and one clerk and interpreter to each corps. The corps should be split up into ten companies, each under a chief or native of importance. Each company should be again sub-divided into gangs of from twenty to twenty-five men, each having its head man. A corps will consist of, therefore—

    1 British Officer.
    1 ,,   Non-commissioned Officer.
    1 Native Clerk and Interpreter.
   10 ,,   Chiefs, or " Bigmen."
  20 Headmen.
 500 Carriers.

Corps should have distinctive colours—a broad band of cloth worn round the arm—the chiefs being distinguished by a particular head-dress, and the headmen of gangs carrying flags of the corps colour.

Take a line of communication from the sea to the advanced depot to be 100 miles in length, and that two corps (1,000 carriers) are told off to each depot on the line, ten corps are required, supposing the distance between each depot be twenty miles.

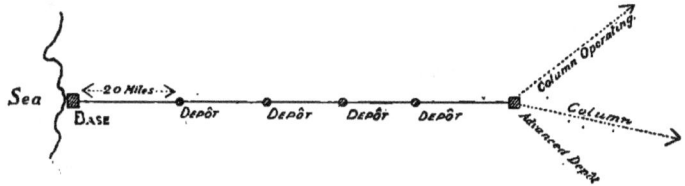

One corps at the base, one at the advanced depot, and two at each of the four depots along the line.

In five days one corps will transport 500 loads to the advanced depot, two corps will in four days place 1,000 loads at the next depot, and so on. Therefore, by the time the advanced depot has received its 500 loads, all the other depots will have received 1,000. Each depot along the line will now send one corps of loaded carriers ten miles forward, and one of empty-handed carriers ten back, loads at the half-way places are transferred to the empty-handed carriers, who return with them to their depot. Thus 500 loads arrive each day at the advanced depot. This method of working the carriers has been found the most satisfactory, for each man returns every evening to the same camp and is able to leave his private goods and chattels in one spot instead of carrying them about with him. Should any section of the line be liable to attack, extra guards of soldiers will of course be required for the protection of the corps while at work. All depots, however, should be laid out so as to ensure safety against attack, and the bush should be cleared round them to give a clear field for fire.

Ashanti, 1900. In the 1900 Ashanti Campaign, some 15,000 carriers were at work on the line of communication. 9,500 regularly enlisted men worked the line from the Prah River to Kumassi, about 74 miles, and these received food, clothing, and a fixed rate of pay. They were guarded by troops. South of the Prah about 5,000 more were employed; these, however, worked at their own risk and were paid by the journey.

Another Method. Instead of giving each corps a colour, there is another very simple and perhaps more satisfactory method. It was used with success on the Aro Expedition. Cheap metal discs, with a hole in them for a string by which to hang them round a

TRANSPORT AND SUPPLIES 113

carrier's neck, can be obtained at very little cost; these can be stamped with figures and letters, each letter having 50 numbers, A1, A2, &c. Flags must still be used for head men, and distinguishing marks for chiefs. A nominal roll at the commencement is made, and a carrier's disc marks and corps noted against his name. Thus the identification of men who misbehave themselves or are wounded or killed is a simple matter.

It is a thing to remember that should a man be killed, his friends and relations in another country perhaps become impressed with the care with which the white man looks after each carrier should identification be easy. D 45 dies of pneumonia on 15th September, and has drawn no pay up to date of his death; his name and country are found opposite the letter and number on the roll, and his relatives receive what was due to him. They are conscious of the fair dealing methods of the white man, and should carriers be required at a future time these relatives can be relied upon to give us a good character. Carriers, as well as more highly civilized human beings, are all the better for not being grouped and classed as cattle.

In 1902, at the close of the Ibeku-Olokoro Expedition in Southern Nigeria, all the carriers volunteered to leave their country and take part in the Afikpo Expedition. They were engaged for the march across country from Bendi to Ungwana, where the new force was assembling. On arrival at the latter place it was found that the District Commissioner had already engaged sufficient numbers for the work from the friendly tribes about. The difficulty now was how to deal with the men, for all were not required, and the men brought from Bendi absolutely refused to go home. Finally it was decided to take a certain number from each

Ibeku-Olokoro Expedition.

tribe, and the remainder would have to return to their country. The difficulty was over apparently, but next morning at reveille when the carrier call sounded, it was found that all the men who had gone off home the previous day were in their old places in column, having sneaked back during the night. At the close of the Afikpo Expedition, when 250 men from a neighbouring tribe were called for to move some stores, 900 came in and volunteered. It certainly pays to treat the carrier well.

Carriers for Columns. The method of telling off carriers to columns is different from that used on the lines of communications. Here, instead of dividing them up into large corps and giving each corps a colour, the initial organisation is the gang of twenty or twenty-five men under a head man. The description of load which is carried is denoted by a certain colour. Say fifty men were required for ammunition, two gangs with two head men would be told off and given red as the colour, the men wearing red cloth round their arms and the head men carrying red flags. The hospital might be blue, kits yellow, and so on. This classing of the carriers by colours is very little work at the start, and saves endless trouble afterwards.

Every man must have a matchet. All the clearing of the bush required during an expedition is done by gangs of carriers shoulder to shoulder in line, protected by soldiers thrown well out into the bush in front of them. It is wonderful to see the dense bush disappear before these lines, and the importance of arming each carrier before the start of the campaign with a matchet is very soon apparent.

CHAPTER IV.

UNIT, THE SECTION.

BUSH warfare, probably more than any other kind, tries the individual courage and resource of officers and men. Small bodies of men are often cut off from communication with co-operating bodies, although comparatively quite close to them. The task of command and supervision is taken out of an advanced guard commander's hand almost as soon as a fight commences. Sections and companies disappear into the bush having been given an objective and a specific job, but once off the path, they are probably not seen again until the action is over. Company commanders in the same way may endeavour to control and direct the action of their sections, but when it is a difficult matter to see more than four or five men at a time, it can readily be gathered that for one man to lead 130, and to really command them in action, is out of the question. For these reasons the section has been chosen as the unit of command for bush work.

This, of course, entails a very heavy responsibility on the section commander, who is generally a native non-commissioned officer. As a matter of fact the captain, subalterns, and European non-commissioned officers of a company attach themselves to sections and all endeavour to work in unison, taking the captain's section as the one of direction; but very often a section gets away under its native commander, and it is wonderful to see what judgment some of them show, and how they readily grasp and appreciate the situation. Being able to talk rapidly, and explain quickly, to their men, in their own language, a desired movement, they are sometimes able to take advantage of a situation which is fleeting. A really good native section commander is invaluable.

Ibeku-Olokoro Expedition. At the taking of a town in the Ibeku-Olokoro Expedition in Southern Nigeria, the enemy were holding the edge of a village with determination; one section under a native sergeant was sent to make a wide détour through the thick bush. The sergeant had the situation explained to him, and was told where to enter the village in rear of the enemy. He carried the manœuvre out beautifully, entered the town at the exact spot within a very short space of time, and completely surprised the enemy, who, caught between two forces, greatly exaggerated the size of the section, and fled, having suffered severely. The village was taken with the loss of one man wounded only. Of course, it is advisable to have a European with each section, if possible, but the above example will show that a native N.C.O. who is courageous, has the confidence of his men, and is an expert bush man, is an exceedingly useful adjunct as a section commander.

Ashanti, 1873. Lord Wolseley found in 1873 that the section was the best tactical unit, and amongst the majority that opinion is still held.

He considered that there ought to be one officer to every twenty men (European troops), and ordered companies to be broken up into four sections, each under an officer. These were to be kept distinct for purposes of command and administration during the campaign. The idea was that

UNIT, THE SECTION

in action three sections were to be extended, while one was kept in support some 50 yards in rear. Although the section is now considered as a rule, in the light of past experience, to be the best unit in the field, still in peace time a company of four sections is the unit for command and administration; each section, however, should be kept complete with its native commander, sub-section commanders, bugler, and proper complement of men. Transfers from one section to another should be the exception and not the rule. A good section soon gathers and inherits *esprit de corps*, and its members boast of its prowess in a fight. Peace Organization.

The French in their Dahomey Campaign made a section of about twenty men the tactical unit, and in Sierra Leone, in 1898, companies were composed of so many sections of ten men each. This is perhaps too small a unit; two or three of these could be put under an officer, however. Dahomey and Sierra Leone.

It is not at all certain that the experiences gained in our South African war and in the Russo-Japanese war do not point to the fact that the section is the best tactical unit for all wars. Should men be employed well extended, no one commander can possibly supervise more than 25 to 30 men in line. Be this as it may, the section is sufficiently large as a tactical command for one man for bush warfare. General.

It is very necessary that all Europeans should carry a compass and learn to work by it. A column is marching north, the line of an enemy's stockades runs, as far as can be seen, east and west, three sections of a company are told to turn the enemy's left flank, the section commanders plunge into the bush followed by their men. The turning movement will have its successful issue enhanced should the path of the sections be directed by compass as well as by the sound of the firing. Unaccustomed Compass.

to the bush, the ease with which some men lose their bearings is almost ludicrous. The firing is often little guide: it seems to a man after a time to come from all sides. He thinks the stockade is to the left, and then wonders what that firing to the right can be, and, oblivious of the fact that he has been travelling in a circle, he pushes on and finds his section and himself confronting the carriers a quarter mile farther away from the enemy than when he started. The above description may read as an exaggeration to a man who has not tried to march to a point in dense bush. Firing sometimes is no guide. The enemy may suddenly attack the carriers from some bye-road, and then the unexpert bushman with no compass is more mixed than ever.

Near the village of Insuta in Ashanti an officer and a party went out to attack a body of Ashantis, reported to be south of the town. Having no compass, and, it being a dull day, he had not even the sun to guide him. He marched in a semi-circle from the south to the north of the town, and there fell on and killed six men of the levies attached to the column before the mistake was found out.

The value of marching by compass was demonstrated in the Benin Territories Expedition of 1899. The Intelligence Officer, who had previously reconnoitred the country, was able to lead a large force by compass straight through dense bush, with no path, for some eight hours, to the town of Oviaweri, one of the principal outlaws against whom the expedition was sent. The surprise was complete, and Oviaweri himself was mortally wounded, while all his effects were seized, and his following dispersed.

Different Races for Units. The practice of mixing up the men of different races, and having a certain proportion of each race

UNIT, THE SECTION

in every unit, is open to argument. The alternative, of forming the unit from the men of one race only, appears preferable. Each method has its advocates. Sir James Willcocks favoured the forming of companies, and even battalions, from the men of one race, and he spoke with pride of the Northern Nigeria Yoruba company, who, under Sergeant Mackenzie, carried out the charge at Dompoassi, and turned what looked like a disaster into a victory, although a costly one.

In India, it has been found that the system of having corps, companies, or squadrons, each composed of a separate nation, works well.

It is a question whether, the section being the unit, it is not better to have two sections of a company composed of the men of one tribe, and two sections of another. In the case of the Hausa and Yoruba nations, the former men give trouble in peace time, and require plenty of work. In action they have great dash, but are liable to get out of hand; they are splendid men to lead in a charge. Soldiers of the latter nation are quiet, steady men in barracks, and carry that steadiness with them into action; but they have not the dash of the Hausa. The two nations working alongside one another in separate sections impart their best characteristics one to the other—the Hausa gives the Yoruba his dash, and the Yoruba imparts his steadiness to his more volatile companion.

Were these nations mixed in one section, cohesion would suffer, and the unit, the section, be apt to become split up. Occasionally a first-class Yoruba is met with who possesses the requisite dash, and he is a man to make a note of.

CHAPTER V.

ARTILLERY AND MACHINE GUNS.

THE moral, as well as the material, effect of artillery against savages is very great. It is only since 1900 that the Vickers-Maxim 75-millimetre (2.95in.) Q.F. gun has been adopted in West Africa; up to that time the 7-pounder muzzle-loading gun was the one employed. As pointed out in an earlier chapter, one millimetre is about equal to three 7-pounders.

The latter gun used to be quite powerful enough for what used to be encountered, but tribes have now learnt to build massive defences. A heavier gun became necessary about 1900, and even with it, several rounds of double common shell were necessary to make any impression on the solid stockades which were found in Ashanti.

As may be conceived, guns, to be of any use, must be pushed up into the firing line in bush warfare. A stockade is disclosed round a bend in the road, and perhaps is not more than fifty or sixty yards away. Guns have to be brought to the bend before they can open fire at all.

Value of Case Shot. The case shot of the millimetre is powerful, and can be used with great effect, even against light stockades.

In the Igarra Expedition, at one place the enemy were posted on the far side of a rapid and unfordable river, which was some thirty yards wide. The only way across was by a slippery log, partially under water and over which the current bubbled. The enemy had the more commanding bank, and

ARTILLERY AND MACHINE GUNS 121

were ensconced in a trench running along the top, crowned by a light stockade, the latter useful more as a screen from view than as a protection against fire. Rifle fire and maxims seemed to make no impression on the savages, who kept up such a hot fusilade that the crossing was impossible. The millimetre was brought to within about twenty yards of the bank, and opened with case on that part of the defences facing the log. It blew huge pieces away and so demoralised the defenders of that portion of the trench that the crossing could be undertaken.

Should it be impossible to bring guns into action, difficulties are always increased. This happened at another stockade the same day; it was impossible to bring the gun into action. This defence was built on the far edge of a waist deep swamp, about 200 yards across, and in which tall reeds were growing, which hid the stockade from view until within about twenty yards of it.

To charge the stockade frontally through the deep mud and water would have meant a great many casualties, so those in the swamp remained still, hidden by the reeds, while two sections, led by Lieut. Ward, Lancashire Fusiliers, made a slight detour, swam an open bit of water, and took the defenders in flank and rear. Their cheers were the signal for the remainder to charge, and by the time they got up to the stockade the enemy had gone.

Of course, should the enemy attack as they did in Ashanti in 1873, or during the advance to Benin in 1897, dire execution can be inflicted with case shot. At Amoaful it was used with effect.

During the operations of the Aro Field Force the camp at Ikono was formed near a few houses. These were burnt, but all the walls had not been levelled, owing to insufficient time, before nightfall.

Early next morning the enemy attacked, and began massing behind these walls. The millimetre fired one round of case at a range of about fifty yards against the walls, and then a section, which had been held in readiness, charged. The charge was unnecessary; the wall had been penetrated as if it had been paper, and the survivors behind it had fled long before the section could get at them.

It will thus be seen that case shot in bush warfare is most effective, and a fair number of rounds should therefore be carried. Two or three rounds of case in rapid succession is an excellent preparation for a charge. The hail of lead, and falling branches and leaves, bewilder the enemy, who can then be got at with the bayonet before he has recovered.

During the Aro Expedition the expenditure of ammunition of the 2·95 in. gun was:—

Numbers of Rounds of Each Kind.

Double common shell	32
Shrapnel	180
Case shot	55
Star shell	60

The above numbers are really very sound to work to, and each gun might carry a proportionate number of rounds. The only kind which is perhaps out of due proportion is the star shell. This kind was frequently used in this expedition on account of the number of co-operative columns; by firing star shell at night notice of their whereabouts and proximity were communicated. On a smaller expedition a very much smaller proportion would be needed.

Position of Guns. In the taking of stockades it has been shown that the guns should come up in line with the infantry, and together keep the enemy employed frontally, while a force is being sent round the flanks. It is

ARTILLERY AND MACHINE GUNS 123

to enable a commander to almost at once begin this rapid fire that guns march near the head of the column; they are of no use behind hundreds of men on a bush path, and take an appreciable time to bring up. A section or sub-section, as considered necessary, should be allotted to each gun as an escort.

In hilly or undulating country, when open or only partially enclosed, the opportunities of using guns are many.

In the attack on Bida a 12-pounder gun was most effective at ranges of 600 yards and over.

At the taking of a town in the Afikpo Expedition, a hill was found which overlooked the approach to the main entrance, and was some 500 to 600 yards to one side of the road by which the assaulting troops would advance.

A millimetre and a 7-pounder took up a position on the hill, and at a range of about 1,150 yards searched the approaches to the town with shrapnel up to the last moment before the infantry assault; practically no opposition was encountered. The effects of the artillery fire were considerable, some of the enemy were killed, and when the white flag came in, the enemy brought a number of their wounded in to be treated by the medical officer; amongst them were a good many who had suffered from the effects of the shrapnel fire. This practice of getting the enemy to bring in their wounded for treatment was often resorted to in Southern Nigeria. It meant hard work for the medical officer and his assistants, these extra cases, but it was interesting; it brought the troops into touch with the late enemy in a most satisfactory and friendly way, and tended to establish at once the reputation of the white man and his soldiers for kindness.

Maxims and machine guns are of immense ser- *Machine Guns.*

vice against savages, especially so when the enemy is given to charging home with cold steel.

There ought to be a maxim gun with each company. Although extremely useful at the head, still the remainder of the column should not be depleted of these weapons in order to keep them near the front. A maxim should be with the carriers, and one with the rear guard, even in a small column, if possible.

A maxim is more mobile than a larger gun, and can be taken up or down the line quickly and brought into action where needed; it is invaluable in driving back an attack, and in restoring confidence amongst panic stricken carriers.

With four maxims, probably the best arrangement would be to have two with the advanced guard, one near the head of the carriers, and one with the rear guard.

To sum up roughly, the large guns should be with the advanced guard, while the machine guns should be more or less divided up throughout the column.

In Boats or Launches. A machine gun in the bow of a boat or large canoe to search the banks of a river or clear a landing place is invaluable. Towards the close of the Aro Expedition, Major G. B. Hodson, of the Guides, took a small force up the lower Niger, and in conjunction with the Navy settled some trouble near Sabagrega. Some of the creeks through which the force steamed were narrow, and the launches were a good deal knocked about by the enemy's fire. Maxims, however, mounted in the bows were of great service. In some cases tall grass growing down to the water's edge was cut down close to the ground by maxim fire as with a scythe, and ambuscades prepared by the enemy rendered innocuous.

ARTILLERY AND MACHINE GUNS 125

The armoured steel canoes, capable of holding 50 men, which were used in the Aro Expedition for reconnoitring purposes, had a maxim and shield in the bow. *Steel Canoes.*

Men inveigh against maxims because they sometimes jam. With special maxim ammunition, a properly regulated fuzee spring, and care in the keeping of the belts and gun, a maxim should never go wrong. *Jamming of Maxims.*

Lieut. Vandeleur, in his book, " Campaigning on the Upper Nile and Niger," says of the advance to Bida :—The maxims " really worked wonders in this campaign, and there were no jams, except one or two caused by cartridges, and were easily remedied . . . . . Lieut. Margesson . . . . . took them to pieces periodically. If used much in one day it was only necessary to clean them out thoroughly . . . . . "

The maxims used in this campaign were the ·45 calibre weapon, and were not as perfect as the present gun of ·303 calibre.

The special ammunition supplied now by Vickers-Maxim for their guns should never cause jams.

The correct position of the maxim or machine gun in square is a matter which admits of argument. A great many commanders advocate placing them at the angles of the square, for they contend, and rightly so, that they in this position protect the weak spot. Savages always try to charge the angles, and should the faces forming the angle be heavily engaged, comparatively few rifles can be brought to bear on the ground outside the angle. But in this position, should the maxim jam, the angle is left practically undefended. *Position of Maxims in Squares.*

Other commanders, and perhaps those with more experience, place their maxims in the centre of a face, and are thus able to bring a cross fire of two maxims to bear on the comparatively dead ground outside the angles ; should one jam or be engaged elsewhere, the other can still defend the angle.

Where the force has four maxims, it is perhaps the best method to place one in the centre of each face ; but with only two, the two foremost angles are the best places, as their fire can then be employed to protect the front and two side faces.

During the advance to Bida, six maxims were with the force. One was at each angle of the square ; the other two were in the centre of the side faces. The artillery occupied the centre of the front face when it came into action against the town.

CHAPTER VI.

MARCHES.

OWING to the unfortunate fact that there is no twilight in the tropics such as we are accustomed to in England, marches have to be carried out to a great extent under the full rays of the sun. In India, in the Punjaub, it is possible to strike camp and finish a day's march of twelve or fourteen miles with a small force before the heat begins in all its intensity; but then the northern parts of India are not in the tropics. This advantage of being able to escape the heat of the day during a march is not possible in the Nigerias, for instance—or, for that matter, in any of our West African colonies. In Nigeria the sun is above the horizon for about twelve hours. It is impossible to begin a day's march before twenty minutes to six in the morning, and in the evening it is pitch dark again at about 6.20. While the sun is above the horizon—with the exception, perhaps, of an hour and a half in the morning, and one hour in the evening—its full power is felt.
_{Power of Sun.}

This marching in the sun is very trying to a white man; it affects, however, natives very little, for the soldiers and carriers in civil life work on their farms all day, or carry loads to market, under the full power of the sun.

In calculating the duration of a march, not more than $2\frac{1}{2}$ miles an hour with an ordinary column
_{Pace.}

should be counted upon at first. With a well-beaten path, and a column which has been operating for some time, and in which the carriers are hard and have thoroughly recognised the advantages they gain of keeping well closed up, a faster pace may be set, but the advanced guard commander should remember that what may seem to him a slow pace in front may be much too fast for the rear guard. A fallen tree across the path would appear a small obstacle, but in a column of, say, only 500 men, each man makes an appreciable delay in stepping over it, and before 200 men are over, the rear of the column is crawling and halting, while the front has disappeared round the turns in the bush path, and each man, as he gets over the log, has to double to close up. This doubling is heart-breaking work, soon wears out carriers, and it should be stopped at once; the advanced guard should step short for some time after passing any obstacle, such as a tree, or a stream, and each carrier will soon learn to make a little extra effort at an obstruction, so as to get over quickly, and neither delay himself nor those in rear of him.

Carriers Doubling

A halt of from five to seven minutes should be made at the end of each hour's march, and the tail of the column should close up before halting. It can easily be seen that unless all keep closed up on the march, the rear of the column will lose several minutes, if not all, of its valuable rest, and this fact is soon grasped by everyone, and keeps them up to the mark. When not in touch with the enemy, it is a good plan for the bugler with the rear guard to sound one "G" when the column is closed up after passing an obstacle of any size; this note, repeated up the column, will inform the advanced guard that they may step out again. One "G" at a halt will show, also, when the rear guard is closed up and

MARCHES

halted. Should, at the end of a halt, the tail be still on the march, it is advisable for the O.C. column to ascertain the cause; and should it be owing to laziness on the part of any soldier or carrier, punishment should be meted out, and all will soon learn their responsibilities. Say the column strikes camp at 5 a.m. and marches at 5.45, at 8.15 a quarter of an hour halt should be given for something to eat, and at 11 a.m. the column should halt for an hour, perhaps, for breakfast. Marching in this way, a force can cover with ease from twelve to fifteen miles by 3 p.m., at the rate of $2\frac{1}{2}$ miles an hour, and be in camp in plenty of time to build shelters, pitch tents, and clear bush for defence before night falls and darkness suddenly obtrudes at about six o'clock. *Hours.*

Some men, especially in Northern Nigeria, have advocated the system of marching up to about 10.30 a.m., then lying up during the heat of the day until 3 p.m., and continuing the march at that hour. Although this method has its advantages, provided that sufficient shelter is found, under cover of which the column can rest, still it means getting into camp in the dark, and the men and carriers suffer as regards their food. The native makes his big meal in the evening, and then is ready for sleep; should he be forced to eat it in the middle of the day he is thrown out of gear, and were he to wait until he has cleared the bush and had his food served out to him in the darkness, as must be done when arriving late in camp, he does not get a good and well cooked meal, and consequently his strength deteriorates. On arrival in camp innumerable things have to be attended to: the camp pitched, shelters built and ground cleared, sentry line posted and paths cut, food served out, water found and distributed, sick attended to and *Duties on Arrival on Camping Ground.*

K

wounded dressed, and very often the next day's march and objective cannot be well decided until arrival in camp. It is unsatisfactory questioning natives and eliciting information by the light of a lantern.

CHAPTER VII.

ENCAMPMENTS AND THEIR SAFEGUARD.

FIRST, as regards the position of the camp, or Site. halting place. An open space in the bush, or one of the large market squares, which are formed in the centre of a populous country about equi-distant from the principal towns, is the best place to choose for a camp. A village or town is one of the worst, owing to the insanitary nature of the bush about the houses. Every small patch of bush is used as a latrine by the natives. It is not always possible, however, to avoid camping in the square of a town in the enemy's country, and when unavoidable the houses and bush should be cleared away, and all refuse burnt. With the greatest care, however, it is not a healthy locality for troops.

In choosing the site for a camp, the best one is a flat table-top, with ground sloping away in all directions towards the enemy. The sentries should be posted hidden, so as just to see over the edge. With this arrangement, should the enemy possess arms of precision and small guns, it is difficult for him to fire into camp, for he must aim to clear the edge of the table-land, and then the shot goes high.

In the Aro Expedition, the camp at Arochuku was almost an ideal one as far as the configuration of the ground was concerned. Towards the enemy the ground fell away down to a swamp, except on the eastern side for a short distance. The Aros possessed a certain number of Snider rifles, and their bullets continually struck the trees about thirty feet above the camp, some few ricocheting down, but no harm was done. The concealed sentries were able to pick off men who endeavoured to get up to the edge of the small plateau, and accounted in this way for several of the enemy. Had the camp been on the level, the force must have suffered from this fire. As it was, the only casualties which occurred was when the enemy attacked and sniped from the level ground on the eastern face.

Clearing Ground. Having chosen the spot for an encampment, the troops with the advanced guard should be thrown out into the bush on all sides sufficiently far to protect what open space there is at the commencement from being fired into by the enemy. A staff officer should then stand at the entrance and direct the head men of carriers where to plant their flags; as the carriers file up they should place their loads in lines near the flag to which they belong, and then, matchet in hand, fall in and await orders as to which part of the bush they are required to clear. No delay should be allowed in getting the carriers to work, and by the time the rear guard arrives, a very considerable bit of bush should be cleared. As the other troops come up they are told off to faces, and relieve the men already covering the working parties there.

Distribution of Force. With a force of four companies, each can be assigned to a face. All the men, if the enemy is active, should be employed to cover the working parties. It is very necessary to completely protect the carriers from harm. Should a few be wounded, they become nervous and the work suffers. Sufficient bush should be cleared to keep the camp itself free from the enemy's fire. His dane gun will wound up to 200 yards. The guns and

ENCAMPMENTS, &c.

maxims should be posted so as to command the principal approaches. Should there be a corps of scouts with the column, these can be posted in a central position to act as a general reserve, otherwise a half company from one face should be detailed, and the length of the face to be guarded by the company furnishing this reserve proportionately reduced.

It is useful to let each section build its own shelter separate from the others, sentries being found by sections, half companies or companies according to circumstances. The sentry line is generally made the line of resistance in case of attack, and by thus dividing up the perimeter of the camp equally amongst the sections, confusion and the mixing up of sections is less likely to ensue, than by adopting any other method.

Clearly defined paths free from stumps of bushes and roots should be made between all bodies of the troops; from the camp itself to each section, one connecting the various sections, one from each section to the groups and sentries furnished by it, and also a path all round the line connecting the groups.

The group system of furnishing sentries has been found the best, with either a single or double sentry, according to circumstances, and depending on the spirit of the enemy. Sentries and groups should make screens, behind which they should hide, but keep a sharp look out. The bush should be cleared for about 50 yards at least in front of the sentries, so as to give them a clear field for fire; farther, if possible, but very often there is not sufficient time to clear as much as one would like for the night. Should, however, the camp be occupied for some days, more bush can be cleared away. Sometimes it is not possible to clear any at all. The same arrangement of troops, however, can be

Sentries [margin]

adopted, companies or sections clearing a small space for their camps, with the groups thrown out into the dense bush in front. Communicating paths are very necessary in these cases. Sentries will probably have to be increased. Some commanders prefer, even when there is plenty of time, to clear just sufficient bush to include their sections in the clearing, and to post their sentries in the thick bush, with the groups beside them. Hidden, the enemy comes upon the groups unawares and is taken by surprise. It is, however, a dangerous method, and may lead to a group being wiped out before it is possible to reinforce it.

Carriers. An important point to note in laying out a camp is the position of the carriers. They should have a camp to themselves to leeward of the European portion, and should be, as a rule, inside the section line.

Camp, Aro F. F. The attached rough sketch of the camp of No. 4 column Aro Field Force explains itself. The island was used as a buffer and screen to make the main camp more secure. The enemy came twice, and attacked from N.N.E., but were not able to get their canoes down the small creek. The scouts' maxim was used with great effect, and the gun-boat searched the bush on the flank and rear of the attackers. The Aros suffered severely each time. A column every day from this camp penetrated and reconnoitred the enemy's country towards Aro-Chuku. Several engagements took place, one being the encounter at Okoroji's Farm, which is described in a previous chapter.

Ambush. Should the enemy be particularly aggressive and persistent in attacking a camp, it is a good practice to send a party out some distance in front of the sentry line, and lay an ambush. If a track, or path, is generally used by the enemy in advancing to

ENCAMPMENTS, &c.

these attacks, the task of laying the ambush will be simplified, and chances of dealing the enemy a severe blow enhanced.

A party should go out at night, and it is as well to push past the place where the ambush is to be laid; and on the return journey, which should be conducted speedily, the spot where the party is to hide can be occupied.

Should by chance any of the enemy's scouts become aware of the move from camp, the above procedure will drive the scouts back, and the surprise can be laid without them becoming aware of what has been done. They will probably be under the impression that the party has returned to camp.

These tactics are especially useful should the enemy interfere with the water parties in the case where the supply is outside the sentry line.

At one camp in the Ubium Expedition in 1900, the river from which the force obtained its water was about a quarter of a mile outside the sentry line. Thick bush grew down to the water on the enemy's side of the stream, and this had to be systematically cleared by troops whenever water was required. The Ubiums usually contested the place energetically.

After having had this trouble two or three times, a party was detailed to lie in ambush at the edge of the path along which the enemy came. The troops which cleared the bush pursued for about half a mile, and gave time for the ambush party to get into position. They then retired hurriedly, and were followed up vigorously by the Ubiums, who rushed shouting into the arms of the hidden troops. One volley at the distance of a few feet and a charge with the bayonet accounted for seventeen of the enemy, who from that moment never again molested the water party.

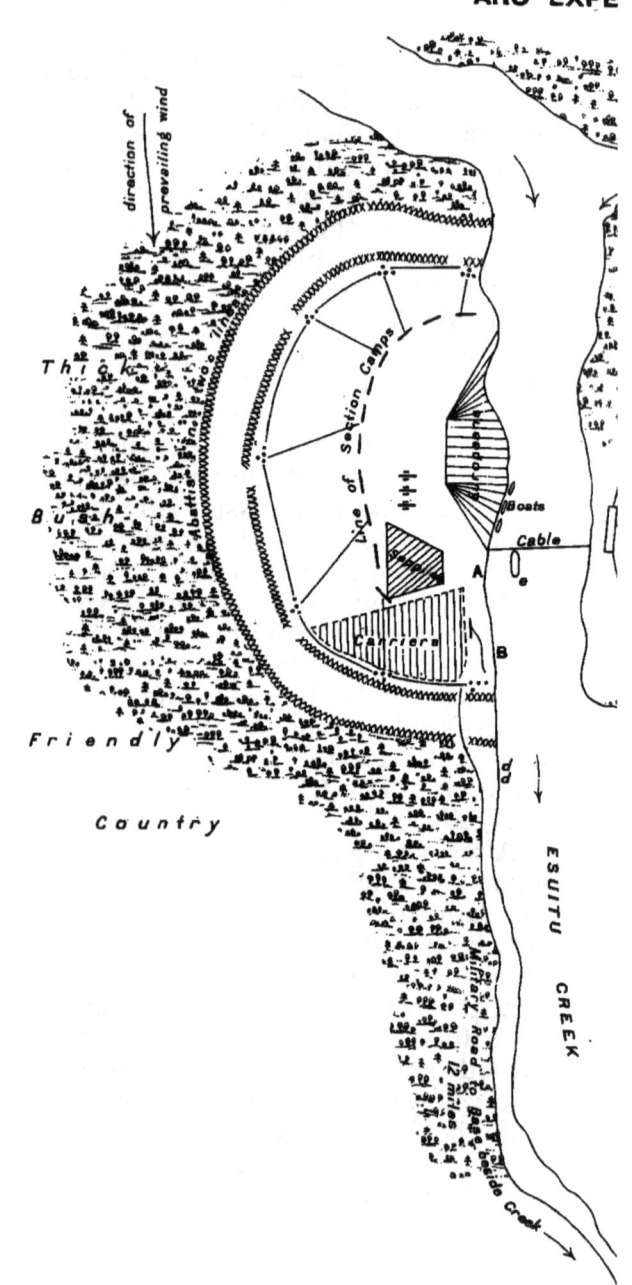

CAMP. No. 4 Column.
DITION, 1901-02.

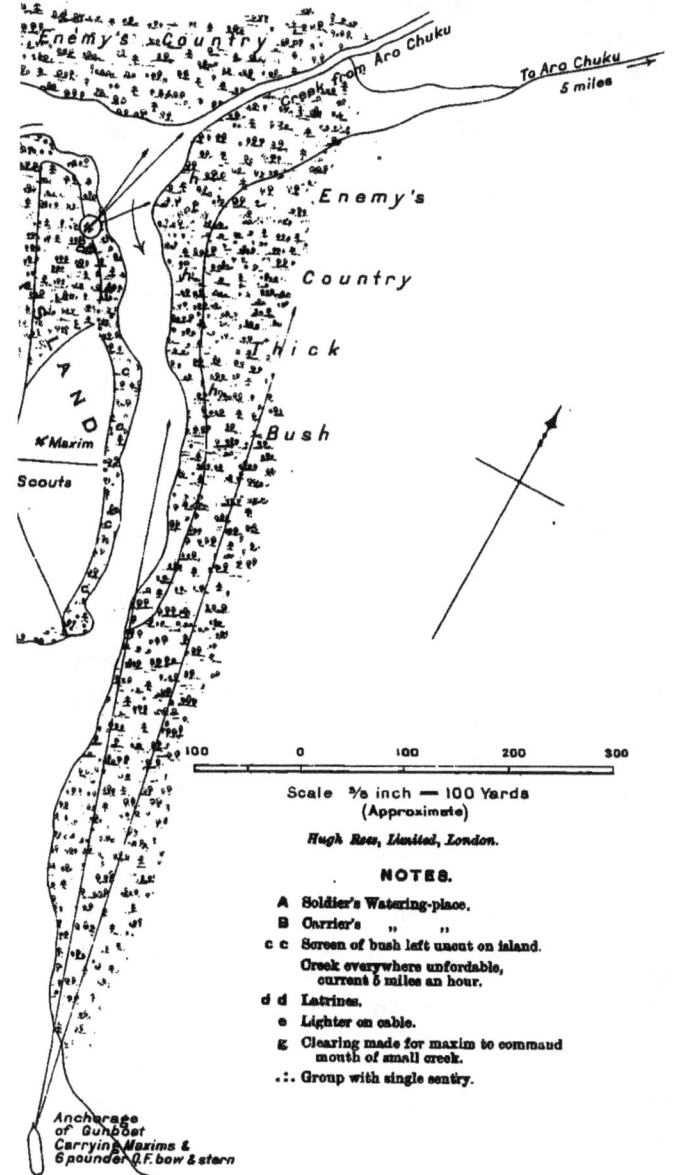

NOTES.

A Soldier's Watering-place.
B Carrier's " "
c c Screen of bush left uncut on island.
    Creek everywhere unfordable,
    current 5 miles an hour.
d d Latrines.
e Lighter on cable.
g Clearing made for maxim to command
  mouth of small creek.
.·. Group with single sentry.

BUSH WARFARE

General Bugeaud, in Algeria in 1841, adopted the method of laying ambushes and so safeguarding his camps, and was a great exponent of the practice.

Fires. No fires or lights should be allowed outside the line of section camps, which should be, if possible, at least 200 yards from the uncut bush, in front of the sentries. Very often some of the enemy lie on the edge of the clearing awaiting an opportunity to get a shot, and a figure in the sentry line silhouetted against a fire gives an easy mark. Fires should be shaded, so as not to show a light towards the enemy. At one camp in the Aro Expedition an officer was going round the sentries at night, and at one group struck a match to light a cigarette. A shot at once came from the bush fifty yards off, mortally wounding a man of the group standing in front of him.

Sentries. Sentries on active service have an unpleasant duty to perform, especially at night. Every nerve is on the *qui vive*, the rustle of a leaf or crack of a twig may mean, in the darkness, the cautious advance of a savage looking for a chance of sniping into camp, as perhaps the prelude to a determined attack from a force collecting stealthily.

Should the sentry be possessed of "nerves" he may let off his rifle, and once a shot is fired it is extraordinary how quickly the other sentries take up the firing until the perimeter of the camp is ablaze, and sleep is out of the question. This promiscuous firing should be sternly repressed. A sentry should never be allowed to fire his rifle without consulting the men of his group and the N.C.O. in charge, who are all lying down beside him. The group system is very advantageous for this reason, and tends to dispel nervousness and promote the comfort and rest of the camp. Should a sentry fire a shot, the commander of the section furnishing the group should at once proceed to the group and find out the cause.

The zareba, or a line of abattis, is of course an additional security round a camp, and is easily formed by the carriers as the bush is cut. This protection is seldom needed in bush countries in which the natives are not in the habit of charging with swords or assegais. For operations, however, against Zulus, or the more warlike tribes of the Soudan, a zareba is a very necessary protection. The French in their Dahomey campaign, in 1892-3, nearly always bivouacked within a line of abattis or shelte trenches.

Zareba or Abattis.

A remarkable case of a camp in thick bush being attacked occurred in 1885 in the Soudan, at the Tofrek zareba ; it is one that seldom occurs, owing to the disinclination of the tribes which inhabit bush countries to make determined onslaughts with cold steel upon well armed troops.

The bush was dense round the zareba, and into this vedettes were pushed some half-mile. Infantry picquets were also thrown out 150 to 200 yards from the camp on all sides. The Mahdists attacked. So fierce and rapid was the onslaught that they followed in on the heels of the vedettes, who, unable to give sufficient warning, pressed in on the picquets, who in turn fell back hurriedly on the main body—in fact, the outposts were of no use. This is a difficult case to deal with, for any large body of troops on outpost would only mask the fire of the main body when falling back. It would be almost better to have a strong sentry line within the zareba, and the bush outside cut as far away as possible and formed into abattis. The time at disposal, however, would regulate to a great extent the amount of work which could be carried out. The above attack was carried out while the zareba was being formed. In cases like this, every available rifle should be told off to the covering troops while the work is progressing. Sentries and vedettes pushed out in front of the general line would appear to be a source of weakness, and are apt to mask the fire in the case of one of these sudde and fierce onslaughts.

In the first Nandi Expedition in Uganda, in 1895, the force employed thorn zarebas, some five feet in height, for protection at night. The Wa-Nandi were adepts at night attacks, and, being courageous, endeavoured to destroy the small force of troops sent against them by charges of overwhelming numbers. This high thorn zareba effectually stopped the charge, and the sentries posted round the inside of the perimeter generally gave the alarm in sufficient time to enable the ever-ready troops to pick up their weapons and inflict severe punishment on the assaulting masses.

During the Bida-Ilorin campaign, the force of 500 soldiers and some 560 carriers generally encamped in square, surrounded by a zareba, if possible.

The square had sides of 110 yards each. Behind the troops on the front and rear faces was a line of tents, and inside these, again, were the horses; the inside of the square was given up to the carriers. Two strands of wire were fastened up round the camp, at a distance of about forty yards, to prevent a sudden rush. Surprise lights, connected by cords to the sides of the square, and capable of being fired in a few seconds, were fixed up, about fifty yards off, to trees or stakes. They burned for about seven minutes, with a bright blue light.

Maxims were distributed round the perimeter, kept loaded and ready for action.

It is a great safeguard, this wire fence round a camp, and whenever it is possible to carry the wire, it is well worth the trouble, should the country be open and the enemy be given to charging home with cold steel.

<small>Wire.</small>

CHAPTER VIII.

Night Operations.

It has been said that night marches and operations undertaken under cover of the darkness are of little use when confronting an enemy in a country covered with dense bush; that, in the first place, the bush is sufficient concealment, and secondly, that the intense darkness of the forest renders movement almost impossible. These assertions, however, are not borne out by experience. Reliable guides and minute and accurate information are just as essential, of course, for a night operation in the bush as for one in the open, but once in possession of the above essentials the chances of losing the road are reduced, and the different portions of the force are not so apt to get out of touch as when operating in a country with less clearly defined roads. The only danger of missing the objective is when forked roads are encountered, or a market place has to be passed through from which paths to all the towns round about radiate, but once set on the road to the objective, the head of the column must go straight.

"Blocking" Roads. All men should be made to "block roads" not used. This means placing tufts of grass, fresh branches of trees, and freshly pulled leaves on the path not traversed. Should this be carefully done by day as well as by night, stragglers can never miss the road.

Guides. Two or three responsible guides (chiefs, if

possible) should be chosen to lead the troops. One man, on the near approach to a town, often becomes frightened and nervous, and is apt then in the dark to take a wrong turning. Two or more together can consult and inspire each other with confidence. Each guide, however trustworthy he may be, should always have a reliable soldier told off to him. A cloth should be tied round the guide's waist, with the knot at his back, and the end held by his guard. A man may sometimes become panic-stricken, or be suddenly seized with fear at the sight of a local juju god beside the path, and, unless secured, will slip into the bush and be lost. His sorrow the next day at his behaviour, when found in his own village, will be a poor substitute for the loss of his services during a critical time.

Information for a night march is perhaps the hardest nut to crack when dealing with guides belonging to a savage nation. The native invariably endeavours to say what he thinks may please the white man, and should the questioner ask in a hopeful tone, "The town is not far off, is it?" the answer will be, "Oh, no, the town quite close, sah." It may take a night march of ten or twelve hours to reach it, nevertheless. When employing an interpreter the difficulty is increased. It is very hard also to get natives to fix their attention for long on any one subject. *Information.*

An interrogation of some chiefs who were good men and anxious to help was once being conducted, and slowly and with great difficulty, on the sand of their village square, a map of the surrounding country was being laid out, and the towns were marked by cocoa nuts and articles from the provision box. After about a quarter of an hour their attention began to wander, and being remonstrated with once or twice, they were finally asked what was the matter. They with one accord said they were tired of this game, and thought the white man might now do something else.

The value of night attacks against any enemy which is not in the habit of carrying out operations after dark is often great.

<small>Night Attack, Ibeku-Olokoro Expedition.</small>
In the Ibeku-Olokoro Expedition, after 2½ months had passed and most of the towns had submitted, there remained two sections of the country in which the fighting men could not be got at, and who had begun a sort of guerilla warfare. Information was obtained that each night a band of these warriors were in the habit of collecting and sleeping in the open square of a certain town. After great trouble and questioning, two of the prisoners, who bore this town a grudge, offered to show the road. They sufficiently explained the way, distance, and situation to warrant the chance of a night attack being successful. Three companies and 200 carriers formed the column, the latter for the purpose of carrying goats and food back to camp should a haul be made. Two companies marched first, then came the carriers armed with their matchets, the rear being brought up by one company. The companies were by no means up to full strength, being much reduced by casualties and sickness. Two guides marched at the head of the column with an officer, one was placed with the carriers, and one in front of the rear guard company. The column marched off at 2 a.m. As it happened, there was a full moon, and so bright was it that in the open spaces of the bush, where the moon beams could penetrate, it was possible to read a watch easily. The moon was waning as the column drew near to the town, but sufficient light was left on reaching the village square to enable the leading officer to see across it, and, what was more,

to make out the forms of the sleeping savages clustered round the dying embers of their fires. The soldiers had been instructed what to do, and silently, with fixed bayonets, the front rank glided round the right of the square, the rear rank round the left, all keeping as much as possible in the black shadows cast by the houses. There was not a sound, and the excitement was intense. The object was to completely encompass the square, then turn inwards, and on a given signal fall on the sleepers, endeavour to capture them, and deprive them of their guns. No shot was to be fired; only the bayonet was to be used should resistance be offered. When the leading men of each rank had almost joined hands, one of the sleepers suddenly awoke with a start, rose up on his knees, looked round, and with a yell sprang up and let off his gun in the air. The soldiers waited for no more, but rushed in upon the savages from all sides. Then ensued the finest rough and tumble fight that it is possible to conceive—sparks, burning sticks, and embers of the fires flew in all directions as the combatants fought and rolled about. The remainder of the sections came up to the aid of their comrades, and nearly the whole of the party, about 50 men, was captured. A great many of both sides had slight wounds, but only one of the enemy was killed, and he had his head cut off by a matchet blow as he was endeavouring to escape. Now comes what might be described as the ludicrous part of the episode. That same afternoon two flags of truce came in, and the two hitherto unconquered sections of the country made full submission. Their reason for thus submitting was quaintly put. They complained, and justly so they considered, against this method of conducting warfare. It was not according to their custom to fight at night; man desired and needed rest, which should not be disturbed, but as this custom had been disregarded they "refused to fight any more." It is not often that one comes across a savage enemy with such clearly defined "customs of war." So rigidly did they and the enemies they had been accustomed to, observe this particular one, that no sentries were ever posted at night.

Sierra Leone Tribes.

To show how tribes differ. In Sierra Leone the Mendis were adepts in the art of night attacks. During the rising in 1898 the most dangerous time was between midnight and five in the morning. They were able to glide through the bush so silently that the most alert and sharp-eared sentry could rarely give warning of an approaching attack until the savages were within ten or fifteen yards of him. Therefore should the enemy's idosyncrasies be studied.

Taking Stockades.

A night march will often be useful as a means of passing obstacles such as stockades, which, held by the enemy during the day, are very often either totally without a guard at night or are only held by a few sentries, who, being easily driven in and the stockades captured, the opposition is confined to open bush fighting.

Amongst some tribes elaborate night sentries and posts are thrown out to protect their defences from surprise, and large war camps are formed just in rear or to one flank of the stockade lines. The sentries give warning of an approach, and the defences can be manned in a few moments. But even here night attacks are often advantageous.

Colonel Burroughs' attack on the Accra Road stockade, about one mile south east of Kumassi, in the 1900 Ashanti Campaign is a notable example of how a formidable stockade defended by a determined enemy can be taken with little loss to the

NIGHT OPERATIONS

attackers under cover of night. Five companies left Kumassi at 8.30 p.m. First marched three companies, which were to storm the stockade and work round the flanks of the war camps in rear, then came Colonel Burroughs and his staff, following them came one company as a reserve, then the field hospital with one company as a rear guard. Captain Loch had made a reconnaissance and sketch of the road that afternoon, and he and his company led the way. Perfect silence was kept, and not until the leading files had got to within about 20 yards of the stockade and Lieut. Greer stumbled and made a slight noise, did the enemy become aware of the attack. They fired a ragged volley, which mortally wounded Lieut. Greer, and then the leading company was upon them. They were completely surprised and lost heavily. The stockade was destroyed and the war camps looted. Lieut. Greer was the only casualty. Not a shot was fired by the troops the whole time, only the bayonet being used. The troops returned to the fort at 11.30 p.m.

A night march on a semi-friendly town will often open up the approaches to an enemy's country and save time, trouble, and perhaps casualties.

In the Ishan reconnaissance to Ulia, described elsewhere, the town of Edelu, on the frontier, was reported wavering, and had the force moved off in the day time to reconnoitre the road through the town, in all probability the Edelu people would have thrown in their lot with the Ulians and prevented the reconnoitring party from seeing the road beyond their town, unless a more serious fight than was considered advisable just then had been undertaken. The party marched, however, at 3 a.m., and arrived in the central square of Edelu before daybreak; sentries were thrown out on all sides and the

Ishan Expedition.

maxim posted so as to cover the doorway of the chief's house. As day broke, word was sent to him that the party had come to pay him a friendly visit, and when he appeared no trace except that of joy was visible on his countenance. Subsequent events proved, however, that he and his people were prepared to cut off the retreat of the party, had the Ulians succeeded in defeating it; further, the return journey, also in daylight, disclosed to view a series of entrenchments made to command the approaches to the town from the Benin side. These two signs seemed to point to the fact that the town of Edelu would not have been reached without a fight had the reconnoitring party been content to start at daylight.

CHAPTER IX.

SUBJUGATION OF A COUNTRY.

FOR the subjugation of an enemy the principal objective at first is his forces in the field. The mere marching into and occupying his principal towns will not as a rule bring him to his knees. The roads leading to his capital are generally the lines along which an invading force marches into a country, and the capital itself is usually the objective to start with, because some objective at first must be taken, until the country is penetrated and his forces found. *Objectives.*

By taking the line to the principal town there is almost the certainty of meeting the enemy in force barring the way and guarding the approaches. The more resolutely he resists this advance on his capital, the sooner will his subjugation be complete, provided, of course, that he is defeated and pursued.

The Ashanti Expedition in 1873, Kano-Sokoto Expedition in 1903, and numerous smaller expeditions, such as that to Nimbi in 1895 (Brass River), Benin River, 1894, (to Brohemie against Chief Nana), Igarra in 1903, Bida-Ilorin in 1896, are examples of sudden collapse after the town has fallen.

In 1873 the Ashantis fought fiercely and did all they could to prevent the troops from entering Kumassi, but once in the town, resistance ceased, and the expedition was over; their power of resistance was at an end owing to their constant defeats and consequent

Kano-Sokoto.

severe casualties. In the Kano-Sokoto expedition, the Sultans of these towns based their hopes on being able to prevent the Northern Nigerian troops from taking their respective towns. Kano fell, and the force under General Kemball moved to Sokoto. Outside the gates of that town the enemy gave pitched battle, and with their defeat the matter practically came to an end. The expedition to Nimbi, in 1895, to punish the Brass Chiefs for the Akassa raid, ended with the taking of Nimbi. The work was all done from launches and boats, booms across the creeks had to be cut and stockades taken, and the enemy contested the waterways to their town with bravery. King Koko fled to the bush, but his principal chiefs submitted and complied with the terms demanded.

Brass.

Benin River.

The Expedition to Brohemie, officially called the Benin River Expedition of 1894, against Chief Nana, was equally short. Nana was reported to have been at one time a slave of the King of Benin, but by astuteness and keen business instincts as a trader, gradually was able to amass money and slaves himself. He was clever enough during his rise to keep in with the local juju authorities, and played his cards with such skill that he was not taken as an offering to the Bini gods by the king during one of his religious orgies. Rising young men who were becoming too rich and powerful often had their careers suddenly nipped in the bud by this potentate, who made a law that the goods and chattels of men brought to sacrifice became the property of the Bini crown. When Nana considered he had a sufficient following and enough money, he left the Benin country and set up for himself in Benin River. He built his town on ground surrounded by swamps and difficult of access. At first he was friendly to the white men, but as his

SUBJUGATION OF A COUNTRY 149

power and following increased, he grew arrogant, and finally his war canoes became such a menace to peaceful trade that the Government had to step in. His town was wonderfully fortified, guns being mounted commanding all the approaches; they were mounted on a light railway, and could by this means be moved and concentrated against any point threatened. With the fall of his town he was captured, and the matter ended.

The Igarra Expedition of 1903, which had as its base Adda, on the left bank of the Niger, was organized for the subjugation and capture of a chief called Adukukaiku. This man had set up for himself in the Igarra country, had established his headquarters on practically an island, being surrounded on all sides by swamps. He had gathered a large following, and lived by raiding the towns of the Igarras and making them pay tribute to him. He became a menace to the European factories established amongst neighbouring tribes, and expressed his intention of interrupting trade. His main town was taken after one day's work, in which an unfordable river had to be crossed by means of a single log before the trenches and stockades commanding the crossing could be captured, and two swamps, each waist deep and elaborately defended by loopholed stockades traversed. With the capture of the town resistance ceased, his followers scattered, and aided by the Igarra people the troops hunted Adukukaiku, who was accompanied by his wives and two or three of his head war men, from one retreat to another in the bush and swamp, and he finally gave himself up.

Igarra Expedition.

There is no parallel in African bush fighting for such a situation and problem as confronted the troops gathered for the Burmese war in 1885.

This campaign is dealt with so fully in other

books compiled for the information of the student who may desire enlightenment on the subject of the pacification of Burmah, that it is not intended to do more than touch on the expedition.

It is an exceedingly interesting campaign, and the account of the fighting, which lasted for several years in the Burmese forests, will repay perusal.

La Vendée.

General Hoche's expedition in La Vendée is another instructive campaign, and deals with the methods resorted to for gradually overcoming, not only the armed resistance in La Vendée, but the fierce anti-French feeling inspired by the acts and methods pursued by the various generals in their endeavours to conquer the country previous to the time when Hoche assumed command.

These two campaigns read together are especially interesting, because it is said the methods of Hoche served as a guide years after in Burmah.

La Vendée, a maritime department of France, had an area of about 2,500 square miles. It was marshy in the south, but undulating and wooded elsewhere, except in the north and west, where the country was flat. A war of devastation had been tried, but had only been the means of stirring up a feeling of fierce resentment against the French.

The French had formed fourteen entrenched camps, within which circle lay the country; columns penetrated to the towns, which were burnt, and the country laid waste. The Vendéans on a signal would collect secretly and carry out some enterprise of ambuscade or surprise; when defeated, they dispersed, hid their muskets and turned into peaceful husbandmen, whose only thought apparently was the cultivation of their farms. Thus were the troops imposed upon, and the enemy, who were fleet of foot and unencumbered, disappeared. No severe blow could be inflicted, and although there was misery, the Vendéans remained undefeated. Hoche, a young general, was at last given command. He devised a method by which the country was gradually absorbed, as it were, by the French. The parts occupied by the troops began to prosper, the confidence and respect of the people was gained, and more than this, the troops subsisted on the country and were in no want of food supplies. This last happened to be a very important point, for the Republican Government at the time could no longer support the force, owing to a ruined administration.

He formed a circular line of very strong posts, and made preparations to advance and gradually overtake the country. These posts were connected by patrols, whose duty it was to be so vigilant and watchful, that no force of the enemy could pass and enter the country already occupied. These posts occupied every town and village and disarmed them. They first seized the cattle, corn, and principal men of a hamlet. As soon as the requisite number of arms were forthcoming, the men were released and the bulk of the cattle and corn restored to their owners; part, however, was kept under the name of a tax, and magazines were formed in rear of the lines. The most stringent and comprehensive orders were issued to the troops, enjoining mildness of treatment of the inhabitants and the immediate fulfilment of pledges given. This line very gradually advanced and left behind it a country at peace with, and even favourable to, the Republic. Acts of kindness were frequently conferred on the people by Hoche, and in many cases destitution was averted, owing to his presents to individuals from the magazines of food already formed. Two columns preceded the line to fight the truculent chiefs, and gradually coop them up more and more. Thus was the country disarmed, reduced, and restored to prosperity, and all at the same time. Hoche laid himself out to become the friend of the people, and especially so of the curés, whose influence in the country was great; through them he gained the confidence of the Vendéans and became possessed of the secrets of the country, which things aided him greatly in his object.

<small>Burmah.</small> To turn now to Burmah. The force employed for its pacification was some 25,000 men. At first the objective was Mandalay, the capital of the country, and this was soon occupied by a force under Sir Harry Prendergast. The country was annexed and the king deported. Now the real trouble began, and is one which is very liable to occur. Before the British could effectually manipulate the reins of government which they had seized, and, in fact, between the fall of one administration and the rise of the succeeding one to full power, outlaws and bandits, under the sacred cause of patriotism, set up their banners and proceeded to loot the country and live the life of robbers. It was against these, and not so much against the ordinary Burman, that the exhausting work of the next few years was directed. The extent of the area to be pacified was some 200,000 square miles. The country was divided up into districts, and to each of the districts, which varied in size from about 17,000 to 3,500 square miles, was allotted a brigade. The brigades were split up, and detachments under junior officers hunted down the outlaws. Gradually the peaceful area in each district grew, the quiet Burmans saw that the British had come to stay, the outlaws were eventually cornered and wiped out, and the country settled down to peaceful pursuits under a Government in

which the inhabitants ceased to be a down-trodden race.

The same situation existed in a milder form in Benin, after the capture of the city, in February, 1897, by Sir Harry Rawson's troops. The king fled into the south-eastern part of the country, but being a "big jujuman" and not a fighter, attracted to himself only a small following, and he was able to evade capture easily. The rest of the country was upset by various men, who either roved about and lived from town to town, exacting wives and supplies wherever they went, or, who, as in the case of Ologbo-Shiri, Abohun and Oviaweri, took up their quarters in almost impenetrable bush, where they constructed villages and lived by exacting their requirements from the towns within a day's march of their retreats. The country was in an exceedingly unsafe condition, markets in full swing were raided, women and recruits seized, and none dared resist.

The process by which the country was ridded of its outlaws, and gathered under British rule, is interesting.

A Resident was installed in Benin City on the departure of the marines and sailors who took part in the expedition, and a garrison of native troops was left behind under his orders.

For several centuries back the country had been governed by the king, assisted by a council of the influential chiefs who lived in the city. The country was partitioned up amongst the members of the council, and each had unlimited power over the villages and towns which belonged to him. The king thus ruled the country through his chiefs, and when he desired his wishes communicated to any town, he gave his orders to the chief to whom it belonged, and it was the chief's business to see that the order was obeyed. Men who were unable to rule their towns were deprived of them, and they were handed over to someone else. By a continuance of this system after the fall of the city, the Resident could reach and communicate with the most distant villages. The first act, however, was to get into communication with the chiefs, induce them to return to Benin City, instal them in their houses and reinstate them in their positions of authority. This did not take very long. As they returned, they were formed into a Native Council, whose duty it was to sit and advise the Resident on all questions. Messengers were now sent out by the chiefs to all the towns to inform them that they must each send a deputation, headed by the principal men, to Benin City, and by this act tender their submission. On arrival they were received with kindness, and the system of government explained to them. They were then allowed to return home, the headman of the town carrying away a submission paper signed by the Resident, which proclaimed that the town had submitted and had been instructed in the new "law." As the deputations went away and spread the report of the friendliness of the white man and the return to power of their own chiefs, so the country came in, until few towns, besides those dominated by the outlaws, remained. Each town submitting had to bring a small tax, according to its means (a few goats and yams). The laws against murder, human sacrifice, slave-dealing and raiding were the principal ones on which at first stress was laid. Each deputation was ordered on its return home to call the people together, and instruct them in their turn. Thus was the whole country quickly taught the ways of the new régime, and what is important, they learnt them through their own chiefs and

SUBJUGATION OF A COUNTRY 155

headmen. In the meantime various detachments had been hunting down and capturing the less influential of the outlaws. The troops were enjoined to treat with kindness the people of the towns through which they passed, all food was scrupulously paid for, and the sympathies of the inhabitants enlisted against the marauders and highwaymen. These methods soon impressed the ordinary quiet Bini with the assurance that the white man had taken the country in order to promote peace and trade, and to put down all acts tending to insecurity of life and property. By August, 1897, or nearly six months after the city was taken, the king was induced to come in and give himself up. He had suffered from his sojourn and roving life in the bush. The Resident had managed to get the information conveyed to him that he would be hunted about from place to place until caught, and that the alternative to this was his surrender, on which he would be put on his trial for the massacre of the peaceful deputation under Mr. Phillips. Whether security in his innocence and in the proverbial justice meted out by the Government weighed with him, or whether the trying bush life after the luxuries to which he had been accustomed, was the predominant factor which led to his surrender, is not known. However, he submitted, was tried and acquitted, but ordered to be taken out of the country for a term of years, in order to learn the ways of civilization, and to give the land time to settle down undisturbed by his powerful influence. A Travelling Commissioner was now appointed and given the duty of patrolling the country, getting into touch with the people, gaining their confidence, and inducing those who had not received the submission paper to lose no time in visiting the Resident and procuring one.

He was given a sufficient escort for protection only. In this way the balance of the towns which had held aloof at first were induced to submit, and the areas occupied by the outlaws were more or less defined, and sketches of the country round, and approaches to, their retreats, compiled.

By 1899 the country had so far settled down and become amenable to our rule, and the complaints against the three powerful outlaws, Ologbo-Shiri, Abohun, and Oviaweri, were so numerous, and in many cases so pressing, that the Government decided to despatch an expedition against them. The outcome of this was the capture of Ologbo-Shiri and Abohun, while Oviaweri succumbed to wounds received in action. The captured chiefs were tried for the parts they had taken in the massacre. Ologbo-Shiri was found guilty of being the prime mover in the affair, and was executed. Abohun was acquitted, and is to-day a leading light on the native council. Thus by gradual and humane methods, and the adoption of a far-seeing policy, the Benin people were brought under control, and the country has become one of the most prosperous and peaceful of the King's West African territories.

Various Methods for various Tribes. It is a peculiar thing how amongst some tribes every town has to be attacked and destroyed, and until this is done, its particular inhabitants seem to imagine that they, and they alone, are able to withstand the white man and his soldiers.

The fact of seeing gradually town after town of their country suffer the same fate seems to leave no impression on the minds of the inhabitants of the unconquered places, except to spur them on to extra resistance as their time comes, and the troops approach their sacrificial groves.

Amongst other races, with perhaps an equal

SUBJUGATION OF A COUNTRY

reputation as fighters, the resistance collapses after one fight, the head men come in and submit, and the country at once settles down, markets remain in full swing, security reigns, and the paths between towns, and the main thoroughfares connecting the principal markets, become the king's highway, and free from the acts of highway robbery, murder, and "seizing," which up to that time had marked so many stages of the road, and given names to the halting places. The attitude of a people depends to a great extent on the power and authority of their juju priests. Should the king of the country combine with his authority the influence which a "big jujuman" possesses, and should he at the same time be young and courageous, his people will, as a rule, fight to the last extremity.

Sometimes punitive expeditions have to be sent against one man, and not against a tribe, as in the case of the Brohemie Expedition.

In others, notably that against Benin City, the bulk of the nation were involved. In the majority of cases, however, the occupation of the town of the chief or king has been only the first phase of the work; after that the capture of this chief is imperative, and the taking of each town which possesses a juju priest with power and influence among the people. This may take some long time, and can only be achieved by going to work in a systematic manner. The best known instance within the last 10 years of this prolonged resistance is the Ashanti rising of 1900. The Ashanti nation is composed of various tribes, and most of them rose; each separate tribe had to be defeated, and their principal towns burnt, before the troops could return home.

Sir James Willcocks relieved Kumassi, and soon after, using that as his headquarters, flying columns visited different parts of the country and gradually overcame all opposition.

Most of the tribes we have been obliged to fight against occupy comparatively small countries, 20 miles by about 20 miles, and in these cases it has been found efficacious to occupy the principal town, within a short distance of which are the main stores of yams and other food stuffs, and close to which there is good water. A comfortable camp having been formed, the bulk of the force proceeds each day against the towns which have not submitted, and should the surrounding tribes be friendly to the expedition, and hostile to the tribe with whom we are at war, the principal men dare not run out of their country. Should these tribes be neutral, and it be the policy of the moment to leave them so, hostilities may be prolonged, but a chief once out of his country ceases to be a chief for harm, and his neighbours soon tire of feeding him, his retainers, and following, for nothing. Ologbo-Shiri, against whom the Benin Territories Expedition of 1899 operated, was caught because he dared not run out of his own section of the country. His towns were destroyed, his hiding places raided, his stores of food consumed, and finally hunger drove him to a plantation, where he was captured.

Aro Country. The objects of the Aro Expedition and subjugation of that tribe and country are worthy of note.

The Aro nation proper lived in fourteen large towns, all within a radius of about 10 miles of their famous juju place, called generally the " Long Juju." Tribes from all parts, some living as far away as a hundred miles, used to send and consult the juju. The Aros were great traders, and penetrated far afield. When any of them heard that people were intending to go and consult the " Long Juju," or ask the juju to settle causes of dispute,

SUBJUGATION OF A COUNTRY

these traders sent in to the juju priests an account of the details of the case, names of deputation, and also specified by name those who could afford to pay most. The members of the deputation were blind-folded a day's march off, and were sometimes marched round the country for a week before being brought to the sacred grove. A voice then spoke from the bowels of the earth, and astonished the wondering applicants by the accurate knowledge possessed. A great many of the members of the deputation disappeared, and were never heard of again; these were popularly supposed to have been sacrificed to the god, but the Aros really turned them into slaves. The power of the Aros grew, and the country about was parcelled up amongst the 14 towns. The buying and selling of slaves was the Aro merchants' chief form of business. Towns outside the area were raided, and slaves procured in this manner, should the "long juju" not produce a sufficient number. Shortly before the operations of the Aro Field Force began, the town of Obegu, friendly to the Government, was raided by the Aros, who massacred some 400 men, women and children.* The objects of the expedition were primarily to subjugate the 14 families of the Aro tribe and destroy the "long juju," then to capture the ringleaders in the Obegu massacre.

The district dominated by the Aros was about 90 miles from north to south, and 120 miles from east to west.

The first objective was Aro-Chuku, the capital of the 14 towns.

Four converging columns were brought to bear on Aro-Chuku. (See Map.)

No. 1 concentrated at Oguta and marched to Oweri.

*Aro F.F. Despatches, "London Gazette, September, 1902.

No. 2 concentrated at Ungwana and marched into the Ahoffia country, cut off the Abams, Eddas, and Ahoffias from co-operating with the Aros.

No. 3 concentrated at Akwete, marched to Oweri, joined with No. 1, and the two marched to Bendi and joined hands with No. 2.

No. 4 concentrated at Itu, and proceeding up the Enyong Creek, camped at Esu-Itu and reconnoitred the roads to Aro-Chuku and feinted towards that town.

All the columns were strongly opposed.

Colonel Montanaro, as a result of the reconnaissances of No. 4 column, decided to advance to Aro-Chuku from the south.

No. 2 column was withdrawn and brought down river to join No. 4, and the combined columns occupied Aro-Chuku.

The combined No. 1 and No. 3 columns forced their way in from the north a few days later. The power of the 14 towns was broken, and although fighting continued for a few days, resistance was over, and the principal Aros began to come in. The Long Juju was blown up and the sacred groves laid waste, while Okori-Torti, one of the ringleaders in the Obegu massacre, was caught. Aro-Chuku was now made into a fortified post and the advanced base transferred up from Itu.

For about two weeks the country round Aro-Chuku was visited and disarmed.

A fresh objective was now taken up.

Three columns were sent into the country west of the Cross River, and were to converge on Akwete; each column was to throw out smaller ones and thus sweep the country.

Column No. 3 concentrated at Big Ikpa Market, on the Cross River, and swept the country between the Cross and Kwa-Ibo Rivers, " covering a front

SUBJUGATION OF A COUNTRY

of 10 miles on a line drawn between Big Ikpa and Enen."

Column No. 2 concentrated at Itu, advanced to Enen, and swept the country down to No. 3.

Column No. 1 advanced from Aro-Chuku to Akwete, and swept the country south to the line of No. 2.

Column No. 4 followed No. 2 a day's march in rear as a support.

From Enen smaller columns visited Eseni and Eket, and finally the whole force concentrated at Akwete.

The third phase of the operations now began, one column (a) was to operate north of Akwete in the country bounded on the west by the Imo River, and on the east by the Azumini-Aba road.

Another (b) was to operate in the country north of New Calabar, as far as Ekpoffia, clearing up the country round Nsokpa, Iba, Alimini, and Elele.

A third (c) was to operate in the Igar country, bounded on the west by the Azumini-Aba road, on the south by a line from Azumini to Abong, and east by a line running due north of Abong.

The fourth and last phase of the operations consisted of—

(a) Column as above, concentrated at Asa, and marched viâ Umobi and Oweri to Bendi.

(b) Concentrated at Alimini, marched to Oguta, Oweri and Bendi.

(c) Concentrated at Akwete, and with the Head Quarter Staff marched viâ Obegu and Aba to Bendi. On the way through Obegu, Okori-Torti and another were hanged amidst the ruins of the houses, and on the site of the massacre which they had organized.

The columns concentrated at Bendi. In the meantime the force at Aro-Chuku had opened up

ARO EXPEDITIO

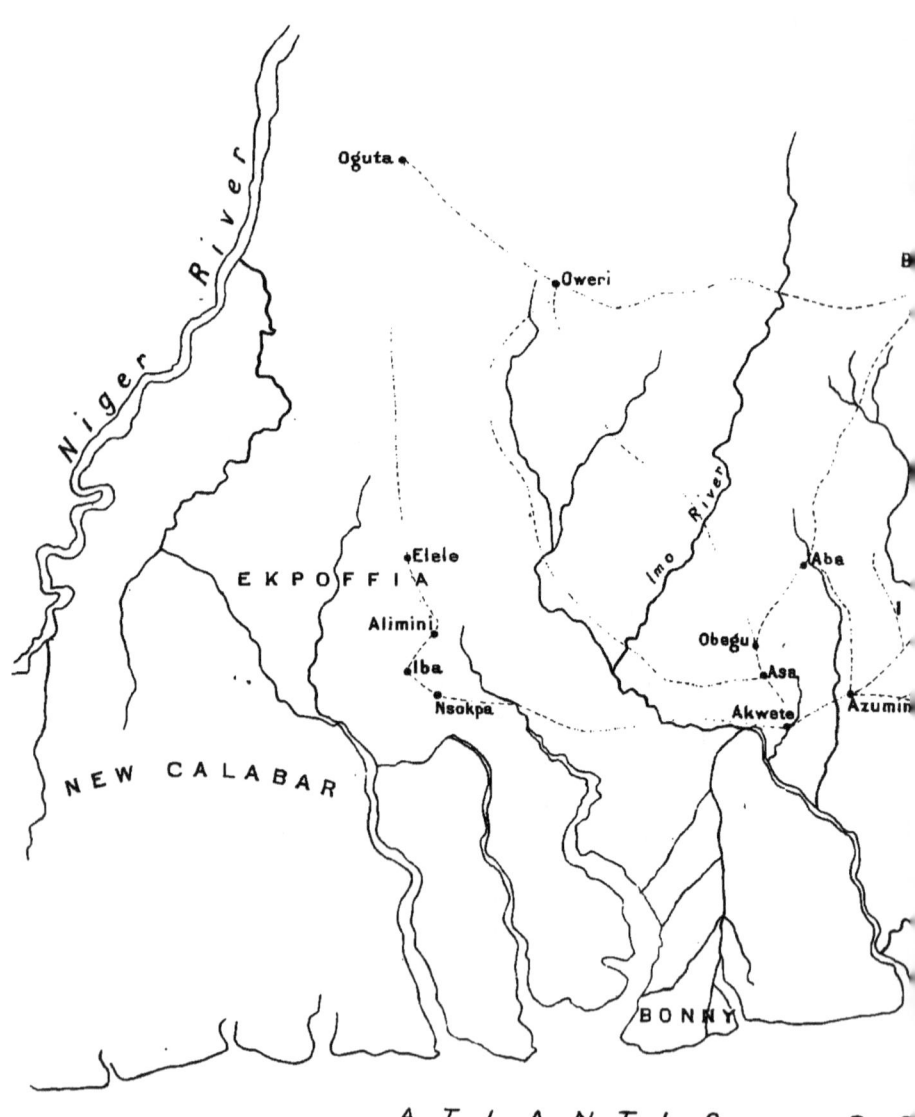

N, 1901-2.

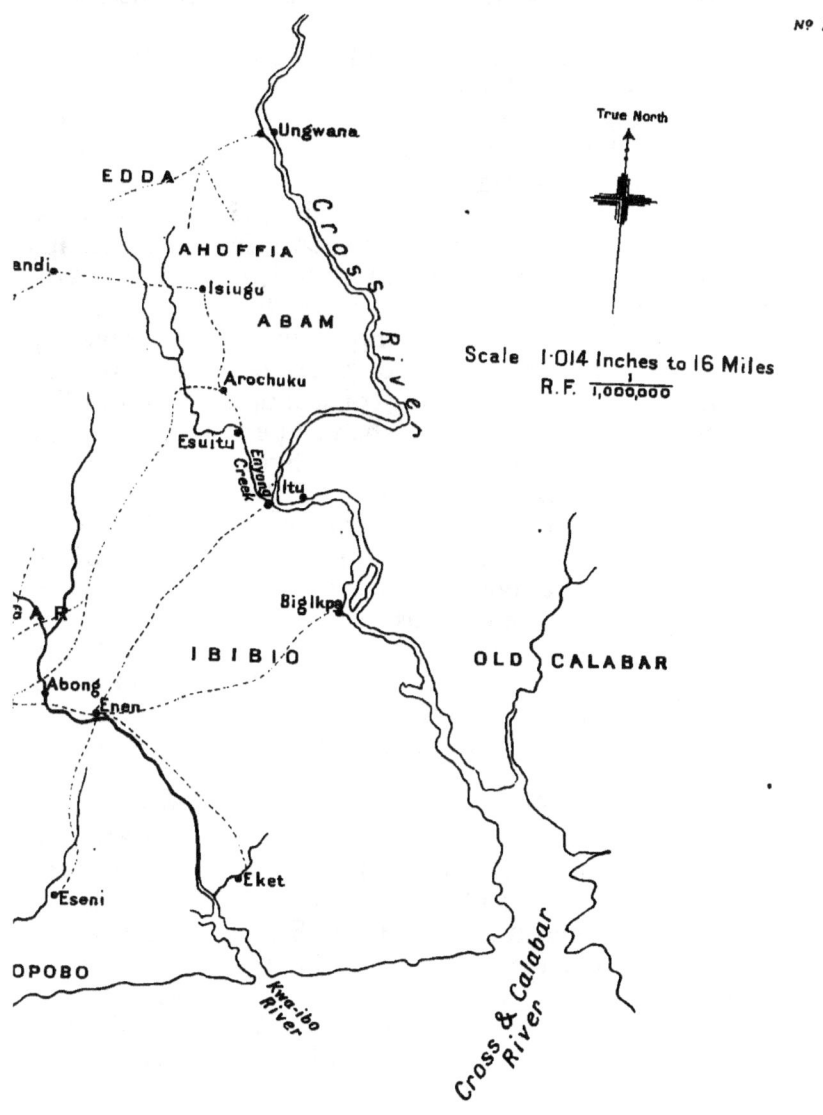

the road to Bendi viâ Isi-Ugu, and stores had been run up.

Representatives from all parts came into Bendi, and here the High Commissioner, Sir R. Moor, held a large meeting, and the Aro Field Force was disbanded. Garrisons were left at Aro-Chuku, Bendi, Oweri and Aba.

Same Methods impossible for every Country. Although the procedure adopted in La Vendée, as touched on above, was successful, it is perhaps unsuited to every country, and in dealing with fanatical tribes. Savage nations have, as a rule, to be cowed, either by having their warriors severely beaten in action and made to suffer heavy losses, as in the case of the taking of Benin City, and in the advance on Ulia in the Ishan Expedition, or, should the nation avoid a stand-up fight, and resort to guerilla warfare, the power of the invading force must be shown by advancing into the most inaccessible and sacred juju parts of the country, eating up the food supplies and raiding rapidly to all points of the compass.

The great thing is to impress savages with the fact that they are the weaker, and that it is intended to occupy the country, enforce the will of the white man, and accomplish the object for which the expedition is organized.

General Dealings. No leniency or half measures are of any use until the savage has felt the power of force. Leniency is treated as a sign of weakness, and half measures as an undecided and wavering policy. When once the savage comes in with the white flag, and it is evident that he desires to submit, the opposite extreme, almost, is the best plan to follow. He has felt and knows the strength and determination of civilization properly handled in war should he be again at his old practices, therefore extreme leniency should be meted out with absolute justice.

SUBJUGATION OF A COUNTRY 163

The savage appreciates to the full, justice, and it is one of the strongest levers we wield. Perhaps the chief hold we have over him, after he has been incorporated in the Empire, is the fact that he recognises that where the white man has set up his Court and abode, there will he find truth, and there will be meted out to him his just dues. He soon finds out also that lies, bribery, and interest, are of no avail. It is a great heritage that has been set up in British possessions, this code of honour and line of strict impartiality.

In dealing with a native never "go back" on your word. Never utter a threat or give a promise, unless strong enough to carry out the former, or possessed of the firm intention to fulfil the latter. Should a savage nation grasp the fact that swift and thorough retribution will be exacted for a misdeed, the work of pacification will be simplified.

Many factors, intervention, religion, arms, the form of courage, etc., are at work when pacifying a country.

In a country held by semi-civilized, or even wholly civilized people (Spanish-Cuban War), although the power and capacity of the invaders to conquer the country must be made manifest, still methods must be more systematic, and need not be drastic, while more leniency and intercourse with the people is advisable. In La Vendée, the first methods, which would have cowed and conquered a savage tribe, only tended to make the Vendéans more bitter in their hatred of the Republican troops, and more determined to resist them. This applied to the Cuban War also. Gen. Hoche's methods would undoubtedly in time have succeeded with savages, but by his methods he took a long time to achieve full success, and they are not suited, therefore, to savages, who collapse sooner under a sterner line of action. One of the main objects of a campaign is to achieve the desired result as quickly as possible.

<small>a Country</small> It is a great mistake to enter a savage country, which is doubtfully hostile, with too great a show of force. It is an error that has been committed often, and generally leads to trouble in the end. A tribe, let us say, is known to be on the verge of open resistance. A large force is hurriedly assembled, and the country is, what is called, "patrolled." This large force does a parade up and down the country, and visits the principal towns. The people are overawed by the strength displayed, and either watch the procession sullenly, or receive the troops in their towns with feigned pleasure. The parade at an end, a report is prepared saying that the tribe is quite friendly, and no fear of a rising need be anticipated. A white man and an escort are now established in the country. Things are apparently all right for a time, and then suddenly the savages rise, cut up, and probably eat, the white man and his troops, and a punitive expedition results. Savages will not open their country to trade, and give up their human sacrifices and slave dealing, at the sight of a patrol, however large and impressive it may be. They must be beaten in fair fight before their country can be regarded as safe for life and property. Were this recognised more thoroughly, there would be fewer cases of white men murdered, and peaceful parties and small escorts cut up. The soldier is naturally the advocate of war, but he does not "trail his coat" as much as politicians imagine. Being on the spot, he generally sees the dangers, which may be averted by bringing a truculent enemy to battle and defeating him, before the expedient of subduing the nation is resorted

SUBJUGATION OF A COUNTRY 165

to, by foisting upon it a white man and a small escort.

A case, somewhat analogous to the above, happened on the Northern border of the Aro country. At the commencement of the Aro Expedition, Nos. 1 and 3 columns met at Oweri and marched through the Ibeku-Olokoro country to Bendi. The strength of this double column amounted to 36 Europeans, 675 troops, and over 1,000 carriers. Everywhere the troops were received with scowls, and in one or two places the natives were threatening, but no open act of hostility was perpetrated. Just a year after, Doctor Adams, the medical officer of Bendi, with a small escort was waylaid by these people, and narrowly escaped with his life. Some of the escort were wounded, while two Government messengers were caught and eaten.

The Ibeku-Olokoro Expedition was the result of this outrage. Its strength was : 12 Europeans, 226 soldiers and 232 carriers.

It took nearly three months to subdue these tribes, and when questioned, on their capitulation, as to why they had not fought before, openly stated that they wanted to fight during the Aro Expedition, but that there were too many soldiers in their country then.

The Spanish-Cuban War of 1898 teaches us the lesson of how not to attempt to solve the problem of subduing a country like Cuba. It was densely wooded and possessed no roads, only bush paths connecting the various towns. The Cuban insurgents were intelligent, determined men, and well-armed. They instituted a guerilla warfare, and one of reprisals ; the insurgent of to-day became in outward appearance the peaceful husbandman of tomorrow. The Spaniards had no plan. Operations were haphazard. Large garrisons were quartered all over the country, and long lines of communications had to be guarded. Columns traversed the country looking for the enemy, who harassed them, and cut off stragglers, and constant executions with their inevitable reprisals embittered the conflict. Finally after three years the United States intervened. Had Hoche's plan, or the method which was adopted for the pacification of Burma, been tried, success would probably have crowned the Spanish arms, for the Spaniards were more numerous and better armed and organised than the Cubans.

CHAPTER X.

LEVIES.

THESE are bodies of men belonging to some Scouts.
friendly tribe or tribes willing to take the field and
aid the regular troops in the work of a campaign
against a common enemy. As a rule, they serve
under their own chiefs, and have attached to them
European officers, whose business it is to regulate
their movements, and as far as possible make them
conform to the orders and wishes of the General or
other officer conducting the campaign. In some
cases, however, small bodies are formed for scouting purposes, a head man being chosen from
amongst those enlisted. This was the case in the
Benin Expedition, for which the late Mr. Turner,
first Resident of Benin City, raised a corps of fifty
Hausa scouts. They were all picked men, roughly
drilled, and instructed in the use of the Snider rifle,
with which they were armed, and were found exceedingly useful by Sir Harry Rawson, who placed
them in the post of honour at the head of the fighting column. It is easy to pick a small number of
men of approved valour from a fighting tribe, and
in a week or so sufficiently imbue them with the
spirit of discipline that, should they meet the enemy
in force, they will hold together, and not scatter and
disappear into the bush, or come charging back
along the bush path in terror, letting off their
weapons in every direction, and demoralising the
troops and upsetting formations. A very useful

small corps of scouts was also formed for the Benin Territories Expedition of 1899, for the capture of the Bini outlaws. These scouts were in many cases old soldiers, and were placed under the direct command of Lieutenant Daniels, a native officer of the then Niger Coast Protectorate force. Under Mr. Daniels this body of levies did splendid work ; he, however, was an exceptional man. Fearless himself, and having natural ability for command, he was able to inspire confidence in his men, who would follow him anywhere. He possessed, also, the advantage of being able to speak Hausa and Yoruba perfectly, and had also a smattering of various other dialects. When the present Southern Nigeria Regiment was organised, and raised to its present strength from the nucleus of the old force, Mr. Daniels was given command of the Scout Company which was formed, and under his leadership the body gained a high reputation. But for even small bodies of levies it is necessary to have exceptional commanding officers—men who understand the native and his ways thoroughly, can enter into his feelings, and can fluently speak his language. Mr. Turner, before mentioned, was possessed of all these qualities in a marked degree ; he had lived amongst the Hausas for years—knew their tongue so well that he could converse with them in the language of fable, a peculiarly difficult and universal mode of carrying on a conversation adopted by these people ; and it is not too much to say that a Hausa would have done almost anything for this white man. His death, shortly after being made Resident of the Benin country, was a great loss to the Protectorate.

Officers To men who have had much experience of black troops the fact will be clear, that the efficiency and usefulness of a body of natives,

LEVIES

whether in the form of regular troops, or levies, depend to a very great extent on the personality of the officer in command, combined with his power of speaking the language. An officer fresh from England may be as fearless and possess as ready a tact and power of command as one who has lived a term of years amongst natives, and has studied their customs and language. The former, however, as compared with the latter, is of comparatively little use for the leading of natives, and especially so if they be levies.

The conclusion, therefore, to be drawn, is that small bodies of levies, in which each man has been specially picked, placed under the command of a man who possesses personal influence with the tribe or tribes from which the levies are drawn, are a distinctly useful adjunct to a force of regular troops, and can be usefully employed alongside them. The adjective "small" has been advisedly used when mentioning the size of the body to be raised, for there are so many instances of large bodies being comparatively useless, and conclusions could be drawn from the actions of these large bodies to show what a danger they might be to regular troops should they be used in front of them. In 1873 Sir Garnet Wolseley sent various officers to raise levies to aid him against the Ashantis, the most notable and conspicuous body formed being that under the command of Major (now Sir William) Butler. It was recruited from the natives of Akim, and was under the personal command of their king. In the end 1,400 men were collected, and they were to advance through Western Akim, and operate on the eastern flank of the main advance. Major Butler managed to get them to within twenty miles of their objective, when they fled and scattered. It is not necessary

Ashanti Levies.

here to enumerate the trials and disappointments which he endured—the title of his book describing his work, "Akimfoo, the History of a Failure," is sufficient comment alone on the heart-breaking enterprise.

<small>Strategic Use of Levies.</small> And still here was a case in which a large force of levies, possessing sufficient cohesion and pluck to even make a demonstration, could have been exceedingly useful to the commander of the expedition. All will admit that large numbers of levies employed strategically may help to divide the enemy's forces, threaten his lines of retreat and cut off his supplies; and that, therefore, by their presence alone, they are useful.

In 1873 there were instances of levies who even before they came in touch with the enemy required a body of chiefs and headmen in line behind them with whips and sticks to make them advance, and it is reported that this "supporting line" had hard work, and that their arms grew weary. Can a more useless collection of people be imagined?

Sir James Willcocks, in his plan of campaign in 1900, ordered bodies of levies to advance along the roads to the east of his main advance. Again were the people of Akim used, and again were they found worse than useless. Captain Benson, assisted by Captain Wilcox, was in command of 4,000 of these people. 250 Ashantis overthrew them, and they abandoned the field and left their officers to their fate. Benson and Wilcox had to fly for their lives, leaving all they possessed in the hands of the victors. Unfortunately, this affair so affected the former, that he shot himself. The courageous conduct, however, of the followers of the loyal kings and chiefs who were shut up in Kumassi with the Governor is in marked contrast to the above. Col. Willcocks' chief use for the levies he had, however, was to scour the districts through which the troops had passed, and so find out their most secret hiding places and stores of food and wealth.

There can be no doubt, however, that the mere fact of having the levies on the roads to Kumassi were advantageous, and had they had pluck enough to advance, their usefulness would have been still more apparent. To place an undisciplined body, however, of this size in advance of the main column, cannot be sound. No light on this subject is thrown by Major Baden Powell's corps of 860 levies in Ashanti in 1895. They preceded the troops, but there was no fighting.

In Somaliland levies were extensively used; some of them, however, approached in their arms, discipline, and organisation more nearly to regular troops than those under consideration, up to this. Nevertheless, even here the danger of going into action with partially trained men is apparent. The Erego affair was due at first to the stampede of the transport animals, and then to the unsteadiness of the levies. Lieut.-Colonel Swayne, in his despatch says :—" The Somali Companies on the left, forming Major Phillips' command, amongst whom were the most recently raised of our levies, disorganised by the suddenness of the enemy's rush, and the confusion caused by the stampeding transport, fell back on the centre and rear companies." Some of those companies, whose training had been more complete, stood fast and helped to save the day, but Colonel Swayne's casualties in this fight were Major Phillips, Capt. Angus, 56 levies, and 43 transport spearmen, killed, while two officers and 84 levies and transport spearmen were wounded. The result was that he had to retire on Bohotle, and the Mullah was left to himself until a larger expeditionary force could be organised. During that part

Somaliland Levies.

of the campaign under Sir Charles Egerton, two corps of mounted levies were raised. One was called the Tribal Horse, and was raised and commanded by Major Bridges, R.A.; the other, known as the Gadabursi Horse, was under Major the Hon. Beresford, 7th Hussars. Each corps was 500 strong. Sir Charles Egerton's comments on the two bodies are :—" These men were enlisted for a term of three months, and though they were undisciplined and troublesome, and unreliable in action, their knowledge of Somali ways, and eye for country, made them useful, though, as all Somalis are, very costly auxiliaries. They were disbanded on the termination of their engagement, and a new corps, consisting of 100 picked men only, has been formed by Major Beresford for service during the second phase of the operations."

He goes on to say that the Illalos, classed as native scouts, a body of men employed under the Intelligence Department, rendered excellent service, and " we have been practically dependent on them throughout for our information, which has generally been good—I may say, excellent."

Then, showing that these levies, who were splendid in scouting work, were not so good in a fight, he says :—" The Tribal Horse, for instance, under their gallant leader, Major Bridges, rendered conspicuous service at and after the reconnaissance of Jidballi, while in the subsequent battle they were most disappointing."

The Somali Mounted Infantry and Gadabursi Horse were suddenly rushed during the progress of the battle while dismounted, and suffered some casualties, during which, unfortunately, Captain Welland, R.A.M.C., was killed.

Somaliland is not a bush country, but there are parts of it covered by just as dense a growth as is found in some West African Colonies, and when in the dense bush, the levies were really a source of weakness to other troops when alongside of them. In the open country the levy and irregular has more scope, and can get out of the way of trouble without the movement being so noticeable, and with less danger of contaminating the spirit and formations of regular troops.

It is not likely that the two leaders of the levies of horse, gallant and capable officers as Sir Charles Egerton calls them, would have considered that their men were fit to stand up to the Mullah's forces, and prepare the way for the regulars which were following them into battle; and still this action is what is expected of levies on a bush path when in advance of troops. One can rely on very small bodies of picked scouts holding their ground when they know the troops are at their elbows, but it is impossible to expect large numbers, 1,000 men or so, to do so.

At all events, experience teaches not to rely on them.

Another class of levy was employed in Somaliland; these were men used to raid the enemy and harass his flanks and rear.

The Ogaden tribe offered to help by raids, and consent was given on condition no arms were issued to them. Capt. Munn, 36th Sikhs, accompanied by another officer and a small escort, was deputed to proceed to the Ogaden country "to give the movement its proper direction." Sir Charles Egerton says :— {Strategic Use.}

"Although Captain Munn . . . . . could never persuade these people, in spite of their promises, to attack any of the Mullah's raiding parties, his presence had a distinctly deterring effect on the latter, and gave confidence to the tribes in the immediate neighbourhood."

This is a very useful way of accepting the assistance of a friendly tribe, and had arms been issued to a small section of them, their value as a retaining and disturbing element would undoubtedly have been increased. Political reasons forbade the arming of them, however.

It is a great mistake to expect too much from a body of levies; it is an excellent asset for a commander to have, but, like all good things, its value depends to a great extent on the knowledge of how to use it.

In this campaign the offer of this kind of help by King Menelik of Abyssinia was accepted. He sent a force to which were attached several British officers, and which operated in the south-western portion of Somaliland and shut off this part of the country to the Mullah. No one will deny that Menelik's warriors were of great use, and served the purpose for which they were intended. It was not proposed, however, to go so far as to ask him to send a contingent to act alongside of our troops. Such a proceeding would have been bad policy, for although they could hardly have been classed as levies, such as are under consideration, still, their methods and discipline would have been opposed to our ideas, and a contingent of these people attached to any column would have been a fruitful source of anxiety to the column commander.

Appearances Deceptive In accepting the offers of help from chiefs, it is very unwise to be guided by appearances. The most bloodthirsty looking ruffians are often the most chicken-hearted.

Ishan reconnaissance. Before the Ishan Expedition, which operated on the Eastern border of the Benin country, a reconnaissance was being conducted.

At a certain town, by name Irua, the chief of which was called Ogirua, it was rumoured that the approach to the Ishan town of Ulia was strongly guarded and intrenched ; it was decided to reconnoitre the road as far as possible.

Ogirua offered to aid with 30 of his most noted warriors, who were to lead the way and find the enemy, should the road be defended.

They paraded for inspection the evening before, and all had a gun and carried a sword, while a great many possessed two swords and had horse pistols stuck in their cummerbands. They looked a determined lot, and the reconnaissance appeared fraught with more danger than was anticipated, should the enemy be able to put a strong force of similar desperadoes into the field. On each man being asked if he was really anxious to lead the way on the morrow, all except one expressed their anxiety to proceed against the common enemy, who had despoiled their farms, and in some cases carried off their women. The one whose heart failed him maintained his desire to go, but family matters, over which he had no control, had suddenly obtruded, so he was sent away. As turned out, he was probably the bravest of the lot, for he was not afraid to back out of the enterprise.

The small column started by the light of the moon at 3 a.m., Ogirua and his contingent leading. The patrol consisted of fifty men and a maxim gun, and was divided into three parties of equal strength, the maxim marching at the head of No. 2 party. Ogirua had been given very minute instructions what to do. His people were to find the enemy, on which they could fire their guns in his direction ; they were then to remain quiet while the soldiers passed in front of them to complete the work; their duty was then to follow on in rear, and on the enemy being driven in, they were again to take up the scouting.

Ogirua and all said they quite understood.

At daylight the friendly town of Edelu was passed, on the border of the Ishan territory. The country was open, but some half a mile on a thick patch of bush was entered. Almost at once the enemy's scouts were found, and at the first shot Ogirua and his gallant band fled, yelling with terror; back they came on top of the soldiers, letting off their guns in all directions, knocking the whole of the leading party, some fifteen men, flat, and upsetting the remainder in their mad scramble to the rear. Two soldiers were wounded, one in the arm, another in the hand, by their promiscuous firing, but providentially these were the only casualties they inflicted.

The righteous rage of the soldiers now vented itself on the scouts, and they freely used the butts of their carbines; a sorry-looking crowd finally escaped to the rear, fled through the border town, told the people the column were all massacred, and did not stop until they were safe within their own houses, some miles away.

Ogirua, who had the mark of a carbine butt on his forehead, and two only of his men remained and went on.

The advanced party of soldiers, as soon as they were clear of the fugitives, and had picked themselves up, drove back the enemy's scouts. They soon emerged from the wood into open plantations, where they extended; the other two parties remained on the road. About a mile on, the line came upon a village which was lightly held, and before re-inforcements could be thrown forward the enemy had again fallen back.

From here the approaches to the town of Ulia could be seen across open yam fields; so, having set fire to the village, captured one or two people and a large number of sheep and goats, the retirement was ordered.

The reports of the massacre had now turned the people of Edelu into enemies, for, like all savages, their policy was to keep in with the winning side. They were on the way to complete the work which they thought the Ulians had begun, and their leading warriors had just emerged from the wood, when they saw the smoke of the burning village, heard the bugle march and the noise of the bleating of the live stock coming towards them, so they again changed their minds, retreated to their town and received the patrol in the market place with every mark of joy at the success of the undertaking.

Ogirua bore no ill-will for the mark on his forehead, and was thoroughly ashamed of himself and his contingent. For the subsequent expedition he sent a fine body of men as carriers, for which work they were eminently fitted.

A striking example of the value of friendly tribesmen is the case of a chief who, with a few men, was following Sir Robert Low's force in the Chitral Campaign. This chief had been previously driven out of the country in which the troops were operating. Sir Robert Low sent him up the Panjkora River to the flank of the real line of advance, and by allowing him to spread the report that he was the advanced guard of the British force, he gathered a large following of old adherents. He was able to seize a bridge and the Lowarai Pass beyond it, and his action aided materially in raising the siege of Fort Chitral. This chief's following cannot strictly be classed as a levy, but to all intents and purposes it was such. It will be noted that, until sent off to a flank, Sir Robert Low kept the tribesmen *behind* his troops.

Chitral Campaign

BUSH WARFARE

South Africa. Levies have always been used to a great extent in South Africa, and as scouts, and for the purpose of gaining intelligence, the Zulu have always been looked upon as the best, perhaps, of the numerous black races south of the Zambesi. In the rising which occurred under Bambaata, numbers of native levies were used, and, unfortunately, in a great many instances, for fighting purposes.

For burning kraals and looting cattle they naturally excel, but unfortunately, when let loose on these objectives, they are apt to get out of hand, and it is an extremely difficult, if not an impossible, matter to prevent them butchering women and children.

For real fighting they proved, as almost all levies do, almost useless. In one place about 100 levies were working round a small patch of bush in which one rebel was supposed to be. They would not enter the bush, but contented themselves with throwing stones into it and calling on the man to come out. The senior officer on the spot remonstrated with the chiefs of the levies, but without avail ; finally he and his staff had to lead the way in, and, fortunately for them, the patch was found empty.

In another case a squadron of Royston's Horse was driving the bush, and the system employed was to place the levies alongside the troops in the front line. At one place the enemy attacked fiercely, and the levies fled, leaving only a handful of troops to bear the brunt of the attack. Desperate hand-to-hand encounters ensued, and the position of the squadron became serious until Colonel Royston arrived on the scene with reinforcements and drove the enemy back. The squadron suffered severely.

Exception to above. While on this subject, it is interesting to note one instance within the last few years in which native allies and irregulars were of the greatest assistance.

This was in the Uganda Mutiny of 1897-98, and the levies were the loyal Waganda.

Colonel MacDonald in his despatch says that large bodies of native irregulars accompanied the columns on most occasions, and "a good deal of extra work was thrown on the officers commanding columns in securing the harmonious co-operation of their allies. That the officers were generally successful in so doing, is very creditable to their tact and good management."

Showing that even the Waganda were often source of anxiety.

The numbers available by January, 1898, were 3,300 guns, and during the operations they lost 185 killed, 341 wounded, or a total of 526. In the accounts of nearly every fight the levies led the way and sustained the heaviest casualties. Colonel Macdonald recommended certain of their chiefs for medals, and sums up by writing:—

"The steadfastness and determination of the Waganda, under heavy losses, and during, for them, a very prolonged campaign, have surprised even their warmest admirers."

The Wasoga was another tribe which in this campaign did good work as levies, and they lost 119 killed and wounded, but are not spoken of with the same respect as are the Waganda.

These must have been very exceptional natives, however, and it is not often a commander can hope to find Waganda or Wasoga to help him.

Lord Wolseley, writing about the 1874 Ashanti Campaign, says:— *Ashanti Levies*

"I found that undisciplined native troops were a positive source of danger in the bush, from the reckless manner in which they fired in all directions."

In commenting on Lord Gifford's scouts in this same campaign, he describes how they frequently deserted him in tight places, how dangerous their shooting was to their friends, and how their commander must have borne a charmed life to survive the many perilous positions his levies placed him in.

CHAPTER XI.

INFORMATION AND RECONNAISSANCE.

A COMMANDER will find that, before the first move can be made against an enemy, he will have a lot of hard work gathering information.

He should find out the lie of the country he is going to operate in, the nature, resources, numbers, and arms of the enemy, the friendly tribes he may rely on to bar their country to the enemy, positions and strength of the enemy's towns, and how approached and defended ; what he may count on in the way of supplies, and where the stores of food are kept, and so on.

It is sometimes heart-breaking work dragging sensible replies from friendly natives, but when unwillingness to impart information and to speak the whole truth is added to natural inability to answer a question in a straightforward manner, the job is, indeed, a trying one, and great patience is required.

Having obtained all the information possible, and placed the principal guides and informants in safe keeping, lest they should suddenly feel inclined to go over to the enemy and give him hints, the work of reconnaissance can begin. *Guides.*

Often a native of the country who is willing to act as guide or informer requests to be put in the guard room, and to be tied up, so that, when the country settles down, he may not be upbraided by his fellows as one who volunteered to aid the white man. These men should be, above all things, fed well, and every native luxury should, if possible, be given them. Their usefulness will vary directly as the size of their stomachs.

Reconnoitring Parties. Very often it is preferable, if possible, to get friendlies, scouts, or levies to do the actual reconnoitring work, and by sending some reliable men with them, verify their tales.

One disadvantage of doing reconnaissance with troops is that the troops retire after the reconnaissance is complete, and this retirement is always magnified by the enemy into a victory for himself, while the garbled reports circulated often induce wavering natives and bordering tribes "sitting on the fence" to take up arms.

The reconnoitring patrol must be strong enough to get away easily should it meet the enemy in force, and along a bush path it is difficult to say what may be encountered from minute to minute. A small and weak party will soon be surrounded, and may suffer severely, and perhaps be wiped out.

Therefore, if troops are used, a reconnaissance with most of the force is advisable, leaving only the impedimenta and a sufficient guard in camp. The real advance and attack, however, should be made the next day, so that the enemy's bombastic stories may have as short a time as possible to affect waverers.

Water reconnaissances. Reconnaissances up narrow creeks in launches or boats are fraught with danger, and the best way to carry these out is to scout the bush on each side in advance of the boat, which can act with its maxim or gun as a support to the scouts. A notable example of the dangers attending a water reconnaissance occurred in the Benin River Expedition of 1894, against the town of Brohemie.

H.M.S. *Alecto* was lying in the Benin River, off

the creek, which led up to the town of Brohemie, distant about a mile and a-half. It was decided to reconnoitre this creek and find out whether it was possible to use it for the expedition, which eventually was undertaken.

Lieut. Commander J. Heugh took command of the reconnaissance. The *Alecto's* steam cutter having been armour-plated against rifle fire, the party set out up the creek. An interpreter was taken who knew the bends, and besides the blue-jackets which formed the crew, Major Copland-Crawford and Capt. Lawlor, both of the Niger Coast Protectorate, volunteered their services, and were on board. The cutter had barely steamed a quarter of a mile up from the Benin River when noises were heard in the bush, and as a place had been reached where it was possible to turn the cutter, it was deemed advisable to do so. When nearly round, an exceedingly heavy fire was opened from a concealed battery of guns, and the boat was pierced through the stern in several places between wind and water by shot averaging in weight from seven to nine pounds. The coxswain, James Jury, and Charles Cheek, serving the Nordenfelt gun, were both mortally wounded. Major Crawford, Capt. Lawlor and a blue-jacket, J. Perkins, were severely wounded, while Smallwood, a blue-jacket, and Commander Heugh were badly wounded, the latter shot in the foot.

One projectile completely disabled the Nordenfelt gun, and the shield and protection were wrecked.

Commander Heugh at once took the helm, and gave the order to go ahead. This was not at once complied with, but a moment afterwards Perkins, with one foot hanging in shreds, got up from where he was lying, and taking charge of the engines, worked them as far back as the ship, when he fainted from loss of blood; the cutter arrived alongside in a sinking condition. A few rifle shots only were fired in the enemy's direction, but the chief gunner's mate, Crouch, with great coolness and deliberation, fired a rocket at the battery, which was so well aimed that a slight cessation in the enemy's fire took place, and this shot undoubtedly enabled the cutter and its crew to get away.

Officers not to exceed Instructions when Reconnoitring. The officer in charge of a reconnoitring patrol or force of any size whatever should be careful not to exceed his instructions, or be drawn off on some enterprise other than the one entrusted to him, unless his chance of success is almost a certainty. He has probably been informed of the general plan of operations, and knows how important in that plan his reconnaissance will be. Should his duty not be successfully performed, or should he be lured off on a side issue, however tempting, he should remember that were he to sustain a reverse, he may upset the whole plan of campaign, and seriously hamper the conduct of affairs, even if nothing more serious ensues. His unsuccessful action may even make it necessary to suspend hostilities temporarily. The thought of this should, however, not hamper his free action, or damp his initiative. He should also "play up" to his commander. He may see a tempting bait which, owing to converging columns and the careful strategy of his commanding officer, is thrown in his way, and which, should he try to grasp it, he may not only upset all calculations, but prolong a campaign. He should not try to take credit to himself at the expense of his commander, who, had matters gone as he had arranged them, would have given credit where it was due. The subordinate should never try to precipitate matters for his own (perhaps) advantage, and so run a chance of upsetting all. The old adage that

"Nothing succeeds like success" is peculiarly applicable to the question in point. A painful example of the unfortunate result of exceeding orders for no real apparent object, and so upsetting the plan of a campaign, is shown by the line of action which was taken by Lieut.-Col. Plunkett's force in Somaliland, and which ended in its annihilation, at Gumburu.

A reconnaissance under Lieut.-Col. Cobbe, strength about 20 officers and 536 men, of which Lieut.-Col. Plunkett's force formed part, were ordered to " endeavour to discover the road to Wardair, and if not seriously opposed, to occupy the wells at that place. If, however, any serious opposition was encountered, the force was to fall back on Galadi."*

A good deal of skirmishing took place in the thick bush near Gumburu, and Col. Cobbe fell back some distance and formed a zareba. Col. Plunkett with most of the force was sent out the next morning to bring in a small party which it was feared had got into trouble. He found the party, and then, instead of returning, went on, for what reason is unknown, but for none that could have justified the action. He fell in with a large force of the enemy, made an heroic stand, and was annihilated, losing nearly a quarter of Gen. Manning's available troops. In consequence, operations had to be suspended, and in all probability this disaster prolonged the operations for over a year. Gen. Manning, in his despatch, says:—

"From information which has come to hand since it is quite probable that, had the misfortune to Lieut.-Col. Plunkett's force not occurred, Major Gough would have surprised, and probably captured the Mullah at Daratoleh, unopposed."

* Gen. Manning's despatches.

CHAPTER XII.

COMMUNICATION.

THIS is a difficult matter between co-operating forces and columns, especially so if the bush is thick and the country level.

Carrier Pigeons.
Carrier pigeons were used with success in the Sierra Leone rising, but not to any large extent, and then, of course, only between a column, or an advanced post, and the base. It would be impossible to use this means of communication between two moving columns.

Wireless telegraphy was tried in Somaliland, but as General Manning says : " They did not succeed in obtaining any very tangible results."

It would have been of great use in many parts of the country where visual signalling was impossible owing to the density of the bush or the flatness of the country.

Should the theatre of operations be mountainous, as in South West Africa, the heliograph can be used.

The Germans, however, made use of wireless telegraphy in their Hereros rising, and for the following short account of what was done and attempted by them in this respect, I am indebted to the journal of the Royal United Service Institution.

Wireless Telegraphy in S.-West Africa.
In the beginning of the Herero uprising, the German troops used heliographs for signalling whenever the existing wire connections failed.

COMMUNICATION

This service was satisfactory in clear weather, except for the drawback that the communicating stations had to "seek" each other beforehand—a feat possible only in case the approximate position of each is known.

It was accordingly decided to use wireless telegraphy. The "Gesellschaft für Drahtlose Telegraphie," of Berlin, supplied the apparatus, which was mounted by the aerostatic battalion. Three stations were organised, viz., two wagon detachments and one cart detachment, the staff including four commissioned officers, four non-commissioned officers, and twenty-seven men. Gas balloons were used to raise the antennæ.

These stations were first used in practical operation in connection with the attack made against the Hereros near Waterberg. Each of the three detachments was provided with a wireless station, and though the men were not very well trained in the limited time allotted, the troops nevertheless succeeded in maintaining a permanent mutual communication. For transmission up to about 100 kilometres (62 miles) recording telegraphs were used, whereas for greater ranges up to 150 kilometres (93 miles) the Morse signals were received by telephone. The latter course was exclusively adopted later on. While the antennæ were 200 metres in length (656 feet), the men did not always succeed in raising the full length of the wire, the drift of the balloon being mostly too small, owing to the considerable altitude of the ground. This obviously decreased the range of the stations. The dryness of the air and the frequency of atmospheric discharges, as well as storms of whirlwinds, were other unfavourable factors. Moreover, the dry cells were damaged by the sudden changes in temperature. The projectiles of the enemy obviously were frequently directed against the balloons, which marked the position of the German troops. The balloons, on the other hand, rendered good service to the German detachments, marking as they did the direction of marching.

The whole of the wireless telegraph plant was temporarily placed out of service in October, 1904, in order to allow for the necessary preparations before proceeding to the new theatre of war situated southward, some time being occupied in repair work. Three other outfits had arrived in the meantime, which, however, were not provided with skilled operators.

As regards the relative merits of the various types of station, the wagon stations are said to be more readily transportable than the old cart stations, which, owing to their great height, are apt to tilt, and do not enable the men to ride on them. On traversing some inundated ground the wagon stations readily passed through the water, whereas the cart stations had with considerable difficulty to be transported across a railway bridge.

Wireless telegraphy has thus proved itself a most trustworthy and useful means of communicating information in warfare, though in the present case any disturbances on the part of the enemy were excluded, for the Hereros were not provided with any similar apparatus. It should, however, be remembered that the difficulty arising from atmospheric influences is far greater in that part of Africa than either in Europe or America, while the country is absolutely devoid of any resources for repairing the apparatus.

Star Shell In the Aro Expedition, with its converging and co-operating columns, it was arranged that columns should try and get in touch with one another by firing three star shell at eight o'clock in the evening, when it was conjectured another column was near. Either the star shell were blind owing to the damp, or else, when they did go off, the bush was too high, or something else was wrong, and no tangible result was obtained. No intercourse naturally could be carried out by this means.

Launches out of sight of one another can carry on communications by long and short hoots of the whistle or syren, using the Morse code. This can also be done by notes on the bugle, but it is a laborious and noisy method of sending or receiving information, and would only be adopted as a last resource.

CHAPTER XIII.

Relief of Towns.

It may often happen that the commander of a force is called upon to relieve a town which is surrounded and cut off by the enemy.

A relief may be necessary owing to two causes.

<small>Causes for Relief.</small> *First*—Insufficient garrison. The defenders of the place, although plentifully supplied with provisions and ammunition, may be so weak in numbers that there is a danger of it being carried by assault.

Second—A town may possess an adequate force for even an active defence, but, owing to lack of food and scarcity of ammunition, the besieged may only be able to hold out for a certain number of days before starvation accomplishes the enemy's desire.

Sometimes both the above causes are at work.

<small>Strategic Considerations.</small> Strategic importance often necessitates the holding of a place, and in this case the town must be held at all costs. Its fall or abandonment might be a serious strategical disaster. There must be no thought on the part of the garrison of fighting their way out, even if strong enough to do so, and the officer who has been set the task of relieving it must be prepared to re-provision the place, and, if necessary, re-garrison it with fresh troops.

The reasons for holding a fort, or town, and the considerations which have to be weighed by a commander whose duty it is to relieve the garrison, are common to all campaigns, and are not confined to those against a bush enemy.

RELIEF OF TOWNS

The decisions which led the garrisons of Sebastopol, Port Arthur, Ladysmith, and Kumassi to undertake the defence of the several places all hinged, broadly, on one thing—the denying to the enemy of a strategical advantage.

Had the places been abandoned, the outcome would, in the cases of the two former towns, have been that stores, munitions of war, a harbour for the fleet, and prestige would have been lost; while as regards the two latter towns, prestige principally would have suffered, and the enemy's forces set free to operate in other directions.

The garrisons were, however, not forced, owing to numerical inferiority to seek refuge in the towns, but were, when the defence was undertaken, capable of falling back from the place and abandoning it to the enemy.

These, however, were hardly the conditions which influenced actions in the cases of the defence of Chitral and Eshowe, or which necessitated the despatch of the relief force to Khartoum to succour General Gordon. *Other Conditions.*

Here the defenders and individuals were in trouble; owing to numerical inferiority, they were not strong enough to force their way through the enemy.

After a garrison has been shut up for some time, the sufferings and conditions often become general and apply to all sieges; food becomes scarce, the force, which at first was strong enough to take care of itself, soon becomes too weak to break out, and ammunition, which was at first abundant, begins to run short.

This does not, of course, apply to all cases. The defenders of Mafeking, for instance, were capable of breaking out and abandoning the place at almost any period of the defence.

Weighing all these considerations, therefore, the commander of a relieving force should make up his mind definitely beforehand in what manner the garrison requires relief.

Points for a Relieving Commander to Weigh. It is obviously unsound to push a large force devoid of stores of every kind into a place strongly held already, but the garrison of which lacks supplies, and it is manifestly impossible to re-stock a beleaguered town with food and munitions of war, or bring relief of any kind to the defenders, unless the commander of the relieving force has a sufficient number of troops at his command to enable him to defeat the besiegers in a pitched battle, and so open the road.

Kumassi. The 1900 Ashanti Campaign and the Siege of Kumassi is especially interesting as showing the different opinions held as to what constituted a relief. When the governor was shut up in the fort at Kumassi with some 150 native soldiers, he sent out urgent messages for relief, and in this general call for succour probably emanated most of the trouble and distress which ensued.

Commanders of troops at once willingly responded to the call, and by forced marches hurried to the so-called relief of the fort. The Ashantis endeavoured to block the roads and beat back these relieving columns, and desperate fighting ensued, but the troops would not be denied; the upshot was that two bodies of men, one from the south and another from the north, with little ammunition, no stores to speak of, and with a great many wounded, fought their way into Kumassi and raised the number of mouths to feed daily amongst the soldiers to some 750, not to mention Europeans, carriers, and a contingent of levies.

The situation can now hardly be called an improved one, and the relief was still lacking.

RELIEF OF TOWNS

There was not enough ammunition brought in to allow of an active defence being undertaken.

After a short lapse of time starvation actually stared the defenders in the face, and the bulk of the force, some 600 soldiers, accompanied by the Governor and the ladies, had to fight their way out, leaving three officers and 115 native troops behind, or about the strength of the original garrison.

The situation was now as at first, with the exception that a great number of lives had been lost, the garrison of Kumassi had been weakened by suffering, and it was only provisioned for a comparatively short time, and that by issuing short rations. Added to this, the Ashantis had become elated by success, and British prestige had fallen to a low ebb.

Sir James Willcocks, on assuming command of the field force, viewed the situation in its true light. He knew that the way to relieve Kumassi was primarily to provision it. This could not be done without opening the road, and to do this, a strong force was required, as the enemy were in great numbers, and had built stockades and entrenchments, guarding all approaches. Again, although he had plenty of troops to have enabled him to brush aside the enemy, and force his way into the fort, as the two other columns had previously done, still, he recognised the fact that when he did advance he must carry sufficient stores with him into the fort to amply provision the place for some weeks. The difficulty was whether he could collect these stores in time. They had to come from England, and then up the long line of communication by only carrier transport. The garrison kept crying to him for succour, but it was necessary for the commander to harden his heart; any premature attempt at relief would only have entailed a useless expenditure of life, and might perhaps have endangered ultimate success. It was found that the garrison could last out on their scanty fare until 15th July, and therefore by that day the troops with supplies must enter the fort. Stupendous efforts were made to get up stores, and were happily crowned with success, for on the day named by the garrison as the limit to their endurance, a force of 1,000 soldiers, escorting 1,700 loaded carriers, fought their way in, and the much-needed relief was accomplished.

The case now took on a new aspect. Being cut off from his communications, for the enemy had closed in again, Sir J. Willcocks could not make Kumassi a headquarters for further operations, and as the longer the large force remained, the less provisions would it be possible to leave behind, he decided to replace the garrison, which had become worn and emaciated by suffering, by the same number of fresh troops, and to march out the next day and regain touch with his communications. This was done, and Kumassi was not occupied as the advanced base until the country south of it had been cleared of the enemy.

CHAPTER XIV.

POLITICAL OFFICERS.

THE political officer, who is so often attached to columns of troops, is generally an officer of the civil administration, such as an Assistant District Commissioner or a District Commissioner, who, having some previous knowledge of the theatre of operations, can aid the officer commanding with advice and information. The various interpreters are in his charge, and his work is intelligence principally. As a rule, he has been chosen as the officer who is to administer the country at the close of hostilities, and is to be left behind with an escort on the withdrawal of the troops.

In small expeditions the soldier in command may be a good deal the junior of his political officer, both in respect of age and length of protectorate or colonial service, and unless the political officer is a sensible man and the soldier tactful and strong, serious difficulties may arise, and perhaps the safety of the column endangered. The soldier should remember, once the enemy's country is entered, that he, and he alone, is responsible for the proper conduct of the operations, the safety of the column and the lives of the troops ; his duty is the defeat of the enemy and pacification of the country.

Should things go wrong and success not attend the operations through the interference of the political officer, the soldier will be the man on whom blame will fall, and on no one else. This is of course as it should be. A good political officer is a great help to a commander, while one who does not recognise his position is a corresponding source of anxiety and trouble.

On the conclusion of operations, and when the commander is confident that his work as a soldier is over, he in most cases hands the control of the country over to the civil authorities ; when once he has done this, the duty of the officer in ·charge of the troops that are to remain and garrison the country, is to place himself unreservedly under the orders of the civil administrator in charge, and aid him to the best of his ability.

INDEX.

A

Abyssinian levies in Somaliland, 74.
Achin War, 1874, as illustrating the danger of splitting up a column, 61.
Afikpo Expedition, 1902-3, formation and tactics employed, 35.
Alison, Sir A., Gen., 22.
Ambushes, discovery of, 2; as an expedient, 4; in the Benin Expedition, 24, 29; in German South-West Africa, 75, 76; as means of protection to a camp, 134.
America, North, bush tactics employed in, 47.
Ammunition, waste of, in old methods of bush fighting, 1, 3, 4; the question of the supply of, 103; statistics as to expenditure in various expeditions, 104.
Amoaful, description of fight at, 20.
Angus, Capt., 171.
Aplin, Capt., 26.
Armitage, C. H., Capt., 62 (note).
Aro Campaign, 1901-2, composition of columns, 64, 65.
Aro country, method of subjugation, 158; organisation of forces, 159, 160.
Artillery, moral effect of, against savages, 120.
Ashanti Expedition, 1873, 20 et seq., 34; 1895-6, 69, 70; 1900, 3, 17.

B

Backwoodsmen, aptitude of, for bush fighting, 57.
Bacon, Commander, R.N., 25.
Baden-Powell, Major, 69 (note).
Badges, distinguishing, for carriers, 112.
Bayonet, the, in bush fighting, 18, 19, 22.
Bearer companies, native, 102.
Beddoes, Major, 62.
Bedford, Admiral, instructions for Benin River Expedition, 1894, 81.
Benin, method of subjugation of, 153.
Benin Expedition, 1897, 24; expenditure of ammunition, 4; dispositions for, 66; formation of columns, 67.
Benin River Expedition, 1894, 81.
Beresford, Major Hon., 172.
Bida-Ilorin Expedition, 1896, tactics and organisation adopted, 34.

INDEX.

Bird-calls as signals, 12.
Black Watch, the, in the 1873 Ashanti Campaign, 22, 23, 24.
Braddock, Gen., in the battle of the Monongahela River, 48 et seq.
Bridges, Major, 172.
Buckle, Capt., 21.
Buée, Dr., 62.
Bugeaud, Gen., his methods in Algeria of protecting his camps, 136.
Burma, campaign in, 149; methods employed in its subjugation, 152.
Burroughs, Col., 144, 145.
Butler, Sir Wm., his failure with the Akim levies, 169.

C

Camping ground, duties on arrival on, 129.
Camps, the protection of, 134, 135, 136, 139.
Capron, Captain, in the Guasimas (Cuba) fight, 55 et seq.
Carrier column, vulnerability of, 11; protection of, 2, 71, 109.
Carrier pigeons, 186.
Carriers, slow pace of a column trying to, 73; as means of transport, 89; proportion to fighting men, 90; for hospital purposes, 101; estimate of number required for water jars, 107; enlistment of, 110; organisation of, 110 et seq.; to be placed in safety pending a fight, 110; working capacity of, 112; distinguishing badges and flags for 112; result of just treatment of, 113; organisation of, on lines of communication, 111; with a column, 114; position in camp, 134.
Carter, C. H. P., Major, 29.
Carter, Captain, 67.
Check, Chas., 83.
Clearing volleys, object and effect of, 2; their general futility, 5; employment of, 24, 25.
Cobbe, Lt.-Col., 185.
Cochrane, Capt., 27.
Columns, on the march, not to leave gaps, 11; merits of small, 60; danger of splitting up, 61; example of the largest practically useful, 62; large, disposition of troops in, 63.
Command, difficulties of, in the bush, 115.
Compass, every European to carry, 117; value of marching by, 118.
Copland-Crawford, Major, 83.
Crouch, Chief Gunner's Mate, his presence of mind, 184.
Cuba, causes of Spanish failure to subjugate, 165.

INDEX.

D

Daniels, Lieut., a meritorious native officer, 168.
Davis, R. H., 55 (note).
Defensive positions, disadvantages of, 58.
Deserters, information supplied by, 29.
Dodds, Gen., in Dahomey, 34.
Dompoassi, expenditure of ammunition at, 3.

E

Echelon formation, use of double, 41.
Edwards, Lieut., 17.
Egerton, Sir Charles, 37, 41, 172.
Encampments, choice of site, 13; clearing ground for, and distribution of force, 132; building of shelters, 133; posting and duties of sentries, 133, 136; position of carriers, 134; protection by means of ambuscades, 134, 135; fires and lights, 136; in square formation, 138; wire protection, 139.
Esprit de Corps, native, 105.
Europeans, carriers required by, 93, 96; rations for, 93 et seq.; all, to carry a compass, 117.
Explosives, use of, 26.

F

Festing, Lieut.-Col., 64, 65.
Field guns, employment of, 12, 17, 19, 20, 25, 27; carriers required for, and order of march, 92.
Fire discipline, 105.
Fires in encampments, 136.
Flags, distinguishing, for carriers, 112.
Flankers, use of, 12; method of employment, 13, 14.
Flank movements in bush warfare, 27, 42.
Food, capture or destruction of, 29, 31; boxes containing one week's, 93, 97, 98.
French system of savage warfare, 41; in Dahomey, 117.
Friendlies, use of, 80.

G

Gage, Lieut.-Col., in the battle of the Monongahela River, 49, 51.
German operations in South-West Africa, 74.
Gifford, Lord, 21.
Glasenapp, Major von, 75.
Gough, Major, 185.
Grayson, Capt., 19.
Greer, Capt., 62, 64, 145.

Guasimas (Cuba), skilful tactics pursued by the Americans, 55 et seq.
Guides in night operations, 140.
Gun ammunition, expenditure of, in Aro Expedition, 122.
Guns, field and maxim, employment of, 12, 17, 18, 19, 25; carriers required for, 92; position of, in a fight, 120, 122; necessity for a supply of, 121.

H

Halket, Sir Peter, in the battle of the Monongahela River, 51.
Halts, precautions on, 14; object and frequency of, 128; temporary, scouts or sentries to be at once thrown out into the bush, 44.
Hamilton, Sir Bruce, 24, 68.
Heneker, Major, 65.
Heugh, J., Lieut.-Commander R.N., 183.
Hoche, Gen., operations in La Vendée, 150, 163, 166.
Hodson, G. B., Major, 124.
Hogg, Major, 105.
Hospital, carriers for, 101.

I

Ibeku-Olokoro Expedition, 18.
Indirect fire facilitated by a man in a tree, 15, 16.
Individual action the basis of modern bush tactics, 6.
Information, supplied by deserters, 29; difficulty of obtaining reliable, 141, 181.
Ishan Expedition 1901, 30.

J

Jackson, A. T., Capt., 64.
Jidballi, battle of, 37, 38.
Jury, James, 183.

K

Kano, description of defences of, 32.
Kano-Sokoto Expedition, measures for the capture of Sokoto, 38, 39.
Karsi, taking of stockade near, 26.
Kemball, Gen., 28, 38.
Kenna, Lieut.-Col., 37, 38.
Kintampo, description of stockades encountered at, 9.
Kokofu Expedition, formation of column, 62.
Kumassi, expenditure of ammunition in 1900 relief of, 3.

L

Landing at Benin, instructions for the, 83.

INDEX.

Langstaff, Dr., 62.
La Vendée, Hoche's methods for its subjugation, 150.
Law, Sir Robert, 177.
Lawlor, Capt., 183.
Leutwein, Col., 75.
Levies, native, uncertain quality of, 109; advantage of organisation in small bodies, 169; strategic use of, 170; in Somaliland, 171; in South Africa, 178; in Uganda, 179.
Lines of communication transport, 110 et seq.
Loch, Capt., 145.

M

MacDonald, Col., 179.
Macdonnell, Lieut., 19.
M'Gill, Capt., 66.
Mackenzie, A. M. N., Major, 64, 105.
Mackenzie, Col.-Sergt., gallantry of, at Dompoassi, 3.
Manning, Gen., 185.
March, disposition of troops on the, 63; order of, of a large force, 70, 72; order of, of carriers to field guns, 92.
Marching, by compass, 118; effect of obstacles met, 128; average rate of, 127.
Margesson, Lieut., 125.
Marshal, Col., 10.
Maxim guns, employment of, 12, 17, 19, 25, 27; carriers required for, 92; value of, against savages, 123; distribution of, in a column, 124; in boats or launches, 124; jamming of, 125; position in squares, 125; position in encampments, 138.
Mellis, Major, 17, 62, 63, 64.
Merrick, Major, 105.
Monongahela River, inept British tactics during the battle of the, 48 et seq.
Monck-Mason, Capt., 62.
Montanaro, A. F., Col., 62, 63, 64, 65, 70, 101, 104, 105, 160.
Moor, Sir R. 162.
Morland, Col., 39, 62.
Mounted Infantry, employment of, 28, 33, 37, 38, 40, 172; in German South-West Africa, 77.
Mullins, W. B., Major, 37.
Munn, Capt., 173.

N

Native soldier, the, his sense of responsib;lity, 6; not a mere machine, 6; his value as a section commander, 116.

Natives, their method of reasoning, 5; are apt pupils in the school of war, 7, 30; their skill in constructing field defences, 8, 9, 10; their agility in tree climbing, 15; their excitability, 16; their sniping propensities, 29; their treachery, 30; in inland districts, characteristics, armament, and tactics, 32; apt to play a waiting game, 36; their customs of war worth studying, 45.
Neal, Capt., 62.
Nigeria, Northern, topography of, and tactics in, 33; conditions as to water, food, &c., 108.
Night attacks in Uganda, 138.
Night operations, native general aversion to, 45; precautions at road points, 140; guides, 140; various examples of, in West Africa, 142 et seq.

O

Obassa, battle of, 63, 64.
Objective, the enemy's forces the principal, 147.
Obstacles, difficult, turning of, 45, 46, 47; as affecting marches, 128.
O'Callaghan, Capt., R.N., 66.
Officers, qualifications required by, for command of native troops, 168; not to exceed instructions when reconnoitring, 184; consequences of disregard, 185; relative status, duties, and responsibilities of political and military, 195.
Okoroji's Farm, engagement at, 8.
Ologbo Shiri, expedition against, 29.
Onor, fight outside the town of, 18.
O'Riordan, Capt., 105.

P

Paths, cutting of, during an advance, 42; advantage accruing to enemy by knowledge of, 79.
Pekki Stockade, taking of the, 17.
Perkins, J., 183.
Phillips, Major, 171.
Phillips, Lieut., 18.
Phillips, Mr., 66.
Plunkett, Lt.-Col., 185.
Political officer, status and duties of, 195.

R

Rations, one day's always to be on the person, 71; scale and packing of, for carrier transport, 94, 95; for natives, 99; inportance of careful packing, 100.
Rawson, Admiral, 24, 66.

INDEX.

Read, Capt., 27.
Reconnoitring, by river or creek, 182; advantage of employing independent natives in, 182.
Retirement after a rconnaissance, bad impression created by, 182.
Retreat, cutting off the enemy's line of, 42.
Roberts, Lord, his instructions for operations in Burma, 43.
Rockets, employment of, 20.
Roosevelt, Col., at Guasimas (Cuba), 55 et seq.

S

St. Hill, Capt., 162.
Scouts, qualifications of, 12; corps of, their methods and scope, 12, 13; to be at once thrown out into the bush on a halt occurring, 44; irregular or native, the employment of, 167, 182.
Sentries, to remain motionless, 14; posting of, in encampments, 133.
Shelters in encampments, 133.
Shortland, Lieut., 62.
Signals, bird-call, 12; by whistle, 12; by star shell, 188; by steam whistle, 189; by syren, 189.
Sikhs, gallantry of, at Obassa, 64.
Silence, importance of, 13.
Sinclair, Sir John, in the battle of the Monongahela River, 49.
Size of columns, advantages of dividing forces into several small bodies, 60; example of the largest practically useful, 162.
Sniping, 29.
Sokoto, measures for the capture of, 38, 39.
Square, elastic, definition of term, 34; example of use of, 37.
Square formations, 20, 23, 35, 36, 39.
Star Shell as a means of communication, 188.
Stockades, 9, 10; usual location, 10; description of various, 9, 10; attack of, 17, 18, 19, 25; best method of taking, 42; in night operations, 144.
Subjugation of a district, methods employed, 147 et seq.; different methods for different tribes or countries, 156, 162.
Supply, difficulty of, 86.
Supply column, position and comparative safety of, 71.
Swayne, Col., 171.

T

Tactics in bush warfare, waste of ammunition entailed by old methods, 1, 3, 4; difficulty of effective control, 2;

present methods based on individual action, 6; higher training required, 6; example of successful, 16 et seq.; example of combination of old methods and of new, 28; in inland districts, 32; only offensive can be successful, 35; subject to modification in particular cases, 37; "slimness" the essence of bush tactics, 59.
Tighe, Capt., 62.
Towns, walled, attack of, 40; effect of the taking of the principal, 147; examples, 147; relief of, 190; points to consider, 192.
Transport, difficulties of, 86; means of, 86; on East Coast of Africa, 88; in Somaliland, 88; on lines of communication, 110 et seq.; with columns, 114.
Treachery, native, 30.
Tree climbers, employment of, 15.
Trenches, skill of natives in constructing, 8, 9; attack of, 8, 19.
Trotha, Gen. von, 77, 78.
Turning difficult obstacles, 45, 46, 47.

V

Vandeleur, Lieut., 125.

W

Waggoner, Capt., in the battle of the Monongahela River, 52.
Walled towns, system of attack of, 40.
Wallis, Capt., 10.
Water difficulties of supply, 5, 68, 135; carriage of, 107.
Welland, Capt., 172.
Wheeler, Gen., 55.
Whistle, the, its use in the bush, 12; steam, signals by, 189.
Wilcox, Capt., 170.
Wilkinson, Col., 17.
Willcocks, Sir James, 9, 17, 46, 63, 64, 157, 170, 193, 194.
Wire protection for camps, 139.
Wireless telegraphy, 186.
Wolseley, Lord, quoted, 20, 179.
Wood, Col., at Guasimas (Cuba), 55 et seq.
Wright, Lieut., exploit of, 28.

Z

Zarebas, employment of, 28; protection of, 137, 138.

www.ingramcontent.com/pod-product-compliance
Lightning Source LLC
Chambersburg PA
CBHW071001160426
43193CB00012B/1874